THE PENGUIN NATURE LIBRARY

General Editor: Edward Hoagland

NATURE'S DIARY

Mikhail Prishvin was a Russian agronomist and natural-ist. His description of the natural history of the far north-ern provinces of Russia, *In the Land of Unfrightened Birds* (1907), won him the Geographic Society's medal and steady journalistic employment. Following the Revolu-tion, during which his small estate was confiscated, he worked as a schoolteacher in the province of Smolensk.

John Updike was born in Pennsylvania in 1932 and has lived in Massachusetts since 1957. He is the author of twelve novels and a number of collections of short stories, poems, and critical essays.

NATURE'S DIARY

MIKHAIL PRISHVIN

Translated from the Russian by
L. Navrozov

INTRODUCTION BY JOHN UPDIKE

PENGUIN BOOKS

PENGUIN BOOKS
Viking Penguin Inc., 40 West 23rd Street,
New York, New York 10010, U.S.A.
Penguin Books Ltd, Harmondsworth,
Middlesex, England
Penguin Books Australia Ltd, Ringwood,
Victoria, Australia
Penguin Books Canada Limited, 2801 John Street
Markham, Ontario, Canada L3R 1B4
Penguin Books (N.Z.) Ltd, 182–190 Wairau Road,
Auckland 10, New Zealand

First published in Moscow by
Foreign Languages Publishing House 1958
This edition with an introduction by
John Updike first published in the
United States of America by Penguin Books 1987
Published simultaneously in Canada

Introduction copyright © John Updike, 1987
All rights reserved

LIBRARY OF CONGRESS CATALOGING IN PUBLICATION DATA
Prishvin, Mikhail Mikhaĭlovich, 1873–1954.
Nature's diary.
Translation of: Kalendar prirody.
1. Natural history—Soviet Union. 2. Seasons—
Soviet Union. I. Navrozov, Lev. II. Title.
QH161.P72313 1987 508.47 86-17022
ISBN 0 14 01.7003 0

Printed in the United States of America by
R. R. Donnelley & Sons Company, Harrisonburg, Virginia
Set in Baskerville

Except in the United States of America,
this book is sold subject to the condition
that it shall not, by way of trade or otherwise,
be lent, re-sold, hired out, or otherwise circulated
without the publisher's prior consent in any form of
binding or cover other than that in which it is
published and without a similar condition
including this condition being imposed
on the subsequent purchaser

THE PENGUIN NATURE LIBRARY

Nature is our widest home. It includes the oceans that provide our rain, the trees that give us air to breathe, the ancestral habitats we shared with countless kinds of animals that now exist only by our sufferance or under our heel.

Until quite recently, indeed (as such things go), the whole world was a wilderness in which mankind lived as cannily as deer, over-mastering with spears or snares even their woodsmanship and that of other creatures, finding a path wherever wildlife could go. Nature was the central theater of life for everybody's ancestors, not a hide-away where people went to rest and recharge after a hard stint in an urban or suburban arena. Many of us still do hike, swim, fish, bird-watch, sleep on the ground or paddle a boat on vacation, and will loll like a lizard in the sun any other chance we have. We can't help grinning for at least a moment at the sight of surf, or sunlight on a river meadow, as if remembering in our mind's eye paleolithic plea-sures in a home before memories officially began.

It is a thoughtless grin because nature predates "thought." Aristotle was a naturalist, and nearer to our own time, Darwin made of the close observation of bits of nature a lever to examine life in many ways on a large scale. Yet nature writing, despite its basis in science, usually rings with rhapsody as well—a belief that nature is an expres-sion of God.

In this series we are presenting some nature writers of the past century or so, though leaving out great novelists like Turgenev, Mel-ville, Conrad, and Faulkner, who were masters of natural description, and poets beginning with Homer (who was perhaps the first nature writer, once his words had been transcribed). Nature writing now combines rhapsody with science and connects science with rhapsody, and for that reason it is a very special and a nourishing genre.

Edward Hoagland

Introduction

The Russian landscape surprises the American visitor with an impression of feminine gentleness; rollingly flat and most conspicuously marked by the wavering white verticals of the ubiquitous birches, it lacks the shaggy, rocky assertiveness he is used to. It seems a young and tender landscape, without defenses. When the single-station radio in the hotel room croons and wails its state-approved folk song, one feels no doubt as to what the song is about: the motherland. In the fall of 1964 I spent a month in the Soviet Union, and at the end of it my constant companion and tireless interpreter, Frieda Lurie, presented me with a copy of Prishvin's *Nature's Diary*. The volume, printed in slightly ragged type by Moscow's Foreign Languages Publishing House, was small enough to fit into a coat pocket and decorated with a few line drawings in the innocent Soviet style. Frieda could have chosen no nicer souvenir of her country. From its first pages—from Prishvin's sighting of the first cloud of spring, "huge and warm, smooth and gleaming, also like the unruffled breast of a swan"—I felt drawn back into that maternal immensity, into a climate more embracing than my own, into a stately progress of weather and vital cycle upon a colossal stage, as related in a prose now limpidly transparent and now almost gruff, a foxy prose glistening with alert specifics and with *joie de vivre*.

Nature's Diary records a Russian's love of his land, particularly of the swampy, almost featureless, virtually endless taiga that stretches, south of the tundra, from the Gulf of Finland to the Sea of Okhotsk. Most of Siberia is taiga, but great tracts of European Russia also hold these subarctic forests of spruce and fir and birch and poplar, abounding in wildlife; the observations and adventures recorded in Prishvin's *Diary* stem from a year, the author's fiftieth, spent in deliberate nature study at a research station near Lake Plescheyevo, less than a hundred miles northeast of Moscow. The book was published in 1925. It was composed in the time of Lenin's dying and the murderous struggles for power from which Stalin emerged triumphant and Trotsky an exile; but Communism intrudes rarely into the texture of life by Lake Pleshcheyevo, and when it does it takes the droll form of some raggletaggle and self-important young Komsomol members. The youthful socialist republic was still a world where one could get away from it all. "My love of nature," Prishvin boasts, "has never prevented me from liking beautiful cities and their complex and fascinating world. But when I tire of city life I take a tram and within twenty minutes am out in the open again. I must have been cut out for a free existence. I can live for years in the huts of fishermen, hunters and peasants."

Mikhail Mikhailovich Prishvin, the son of a rich merchant, was born in 1873 on the family estate in the north of Russia. While a student at Riga, he was arrested for revolutionary activity. After his release, he studied in Leipzig and in 1902 received a degree in agronomy. As young gentlemen were in those years, Prishvin was free to indulge his interests, and he travelled throughout Russia, Central Asia, and the Far East, educating himself in ornithology, linguistics, folklore, and ethnology. His first two books—*In the Land of Unfrightened Birds and Animals* (1907) and *Small, Round Loaf* (1908)—dealt with North Russia and the customs and legends of its peasants. According to the literary historian D. L. Mirsky, "These studies taught Prishvin to value the originality of the uneducated Russian and the native force of 'unlatinized' Russian speech." Mirsky claims Prishvin to have been further influenced along these lines by a young writer, the Symbolist Alexey Remizov, whose greatly varied production was "unified by one purpose—which is to delatinize and defrenchify the Russian literary language and to restore to it its natural Russian raciness." While such linguistic nuances can scarcely be conveyed in translation, this rendering by L. Navrozov does permit us to feel a certain raciness in the highly informal organization—an impulsiveness of movement that keeps the reader constantly and pleasantly off-balance as he moves with Prishvin through the year. Almost half the book, for instance, is taken up with spring, the summer section is monopolized by the author's hunting dogs, and the final pages are concerned with a bear hunt that took place nowhere near Lake Pleshcheyevo. *Nature's Diary*, and Prishvin's other rural sketches, achieved considerable popularity with an increasingly urbanized Soviet public; he maintained his artistic independence throughout the Stalin era, and died in 1954, at the age of eighty-one.

The nature he contributes to the Penguin Nature Library seems familiar; we have already met it in the scenery of Turgenev and Tolstoy, Chekhov and Nabokov. The continental cold is slow to relinquish the land—we read of frost in May—and quick to reclaim it, with flurries of snow and a film of morning ice on the autumnal marshes. But the fauna, above all the birds, begin their cycles of procreation in the depths of winter, and Prishvin's swift eye sees life everywhere. Carrion crows somersault in their love frenzy, the black-cocks sing and mate as the icy creeks thaw into song, the cranes and kestrels return, and ducks fill the air with noise. Man, too, is active in the cold landscape: "The snow was frozen hard and powdered by the latest fall. The going was pure joy whichever way we turned." And then the frogs stir, the finches arrive, grass appears, and the first mushrooms and the early flowers, of aspen and lungwort; the first cuckoo is heard, and then the first nightingale. These manifestations of thaw and revival are intermixed, in Prishvin's diary entries, with the comings and goings of men, with local gossip and the lore of pike fishermen, with an archaeological expedition and an ethnological excursion to see a pre-Christian village rite, the Nettle Feast. Nature, which to an American instinct looms as purely and grandly inhuman as an Ansel Adams photograph, is for the Russian interwoven with humanity; this North Russia is a vast and forbidding but long-inhabited terrain, warmed in its remotest corners by the touch of men. In the dead cold of a winter night, a hunter in pursuit of a marten burns an anthill to make himself a warm bed of ashes, and the charred ruins remember him. On a desolate marsh, Prishvin (to his annoyance) suddenly spots another man walking. He participates in an archaeological dig, which finds evidence of long habitation, the skull of a prehistoric predecessor—"more impressive" than he had expected, the skull's color "not the color of bone but almost that of copper or burnt clay," the teeth and forehead perfectly white. Everywhere in this wild landscape, people pop up—more than we can keep track of. The peasantry seems ubiquitous, like animate tummocks or another species of animal, part of the land's furniture and included in this inventory:

> The trees, grass and flowers wore their most sumptuous garb. The birds of early spring grew silent: the cocks had hidden themselves away, moulting, and the hens were fasting on their nests hatching their eggs. The animals were busy seeking food for their young. What with sowing and ploughing, the peasants were more harassed than ever.

Some of the peasant lore—frogs are woken from hibernation by thunder, a mushroom detected by the human eye will cease to grow—is perhaps open to scientific refutation, but the observation that the roach is a lonely fish and roach soup makes people brood would seem inarguable. Prishvin himself asserts with mystic authority: "The orioles are very fond of choppy weather. They like the sun to come and go, and the wind to play with the leaves as with waves. Orioles, swallows, gulls and martins have a kinship with the wind."

Man's interpenetration with nature takes many forms: superstition, lore, and annual rite, as in the Nettle Feast; scientific probing and investigation, as in Prishvin's research station; pantheistic communion ("I . . . sat down on a soft mossy hillock under a pine tree and began to sip the tea slowly, musing and gradually merging with the life around me"); and hunting. There is a great deal of hunting and killing here—more than a modern nature-lover expects. Prishvin at one point steps forward to reassure the squeamish: "There is no need to pity the animal, my kind-hearted readers, we're all due for it sooner or later, I for one am almost ready. . . ." To hunt successfully, one must empathize with the animals, think like them; in this immemorial way Man draws close to his fellow creatures. The strategies of foxes, the scruples of wolves are fascinatingly noted. And the minds of the dogs trained to hunt at Man's side are wonderfully well explored. With Olympian humor Prishvin explicates the urinary truce agreements of competing dogs; with a sense of triumph he psychoanalyzes the feminine pretenses of his disappointing pointer Kate, her nose dulled by two housebound years in Moscow, and rejoices when her nose revives in the naked wind. Nature for Prishvin not only spreads itself externally but lies within the mind of a dog, a fox, even a fish or mayfly. With a hunter's heartbeat he tiptoes toward the riddles of the woods, marvelling at the snoring sound that emerges from a tree full of sleeping wood grouse, and speculating on its source:

> I suppose that the sound comes from the fluttering feathers when a large bird breathes under its wing in sleep. However, I shouldn't swear to it that wood grouse do sleep with their heads under the wings. I am judging by domestic fowl. It's all surmises, stories and speculation, whereas the real world of the woods is little known.

Though he was something of a scientist, there is little in Prishvin's grasp of nature that corresponds to Loren Eiseley's paleontological perspective or Joseph Wood Krutch's biological microscopy. He is, like Thoreau and Muir and Annie Dillard, confrontational in his dealings with the outdoors, and existential, his own consciousness his keenest tool. Nature to Prishvin appears "little known," and the riddles that concern him—how do wood grouse snore? why do the jackdaws come to see off the migrating rooks?—verge on the primitive. He restores us, in an anecdote like that of the old itinerant nurse who successfully pleaded for mercy with the wolves, to the pre-medieval Europe of the fairy tales, when animals spoke with dignity on behalf of their own societies and men shared with all life a single network of sensation and motive. The semi-centenarian is thrilled to be alive, he tells us more than once. His descriptions of days—especially of that magical hour before dawn, which he is always avid to witness—have an elemental sublimity: ·

> There was a morning moon. The eastern sky was clouded. At long last a strip of dawn showed from under the heavy blanket, and the moon floated in deeper blue.
> The lake seemed to be covered with floes, so queerly and abruptly had the mist broken up. The village cocks and swans gave voice.

This freshness, the Adamic freshness of earliest morning, is what one finds in Prishvin; we seem to see the earth being created, and its simplest patterns established:

> The most exquisite and mysterious time of the day is that between the first streak of light and sunrise, when the pattern of the leafless trees just begins to be outlined. The birches seem to have been combed downwards, the maples and aspens upwards. I witnessed the birth of the hoarfrost, saw it shrivel and whiten the old yellow grass and glass the puddles with the thinnest film of ice.

The vibration of our animal existence is in him, as well as those tentative motions of mind whereby Man began to subdue his magnificent, riddle-filled environment. The first inklings of morality, of conscious manliness, issue from his hunter's encounters: facing a bear, he experiences the click of courage; perceiving that "the struggle between the proud free man and the coward was inevitable and needful for it's the coward in us that puts us to the test. One could not talk oneself into bravery as one could not stop the heart from thumping more and more violently. I thought it would burst in a moment, but then came the line beyond which there was no struggle, the coward was vanquished and I turned into a mechanism with the precision of a steel spring in a clock." And death, awareness of which separates us from the rest of nature, is banished by natural busyness: "I am no longer young, that's true, but I am as busy as ever and keep my cup brimming full. And as long as I can keep it so, all thoughts of death are empty." Handed down by a more considered stoicism, such consolation might ring hollow; but Prishvin speaks in the unforced voice of nature herself, and with that characteristically Russian blend of fatalism and exuberance and imparts to us her exhilarating imperatives.

John Updike

CONTENTS

NATURE'S DIARY

SPRING

Spring of Light and Water. The First Drips

To those who observe nature from day to day, the coming of spring is announced first of all by more light. The country folk then say that the bear is turning over in his lair; the sun is smiling ever brighter, and though more frosts are ahead, the Gypsy sells his sheepskin.

January in Central Russia: the lively cawing of the hooded crows, the fights among the sparrows, the dogs in heat, the first mating games of the carrion crows.

February: the first drips from the sunny side of the house, the tit's song, the sparrows building their nests, the drumming of the woodpecker.

January, February and early March all belong to the spring of light. The ice seems to break up in the sky and there is a great scurrying of floes up there, and you can see it best in a large town, watching it in the gaps between the ponderous bulks of stone. At that time I would be working in town like the devil, scraping and quarrelling over every ruble, and when at last, my fight for money over, I would go away to a place where there was no chance of making any, I would be happy and free. He is a happy man who can meet the early spring of light in town, and then go to the country, closer to nature, to meet the spring of water, the spring of woods and grass, and even, who can tell, the spring of man.

When after a hard winter the spring of light comes into its brilliant own, people living close to nature grow agitated and keep asking themselves: what will the spring be like this year? And every year it's different from what it was the year before, and no spring was ever like another.

This year the spring of light lingered too long, and its dazzling snows were almost unbearable to the eye.

"It'll come all at once," everybody said.

People starting out on a long journey by sledge were afraid they might have to abandon it somewhere midway and continue on foot leading the horse by the bridle.

No, a new spring is never like the old one, and that is what makes living so good—the thrilling expectation of something new every year.

Our peasants talk only of spring whenever they meet.

"It'll be over any minute."

"It'll come all at once."

The Cumulus Clouds Are Here

Overnight an enormous snow-drift formed in front of our house —all smooth and gleaming like the unruffled breast of a swan. It was with some difficulty that I opened the front door piled up with last night's snow, and I began to dig a trench, shovelling away the fluffy new snow and then slicing through the thick caked layers underneath.

I was not sorry to destroy the drift, for up there amid the airy floes there sailed a cloud so unlike the clouds in winter; it was huge and warm, smooth and gleaming, also like the unruffled breast of a swan. Here and there the same old visions, ever new and pure, came back with the spring, but I greet them with none of my old mad alarm and see them go without despair: like spring they come and go and as long as I live they will return. So why should I mourn them? I am not a child now, but father and master of my visions.

It's no joke, being fifty: remember what the Good Book says? Till your land for six years, and in the seventh let it rest and recover. After seven times seven it will be your fiftieth year; then take your trumpet and blow, for this is your jubilee.

"There now, boys, up you get!" I shouted. "Give me a hand—my jubilee is near!"

Their names are Lyova and Petya, and they are born sportsmen, both of them. I've nurtured my own passion in them carefully and sensibly: they will never kill just for the sake of a good shot but only for food or to get specimens for the museum. During the closed season from Christmas till early spring they spent most of their evenings at dances in town, getting back to our village at all hours. Lyova has even started a moustache: he got hold of my razor and gave himself a shave on the sly and that helped a great deal, of course. But the younger boy's face is still smooth.

After Forty Saints' Day when the rooks and the larks and the other small birds are back, my boys give up their dances and start getting ready for blackcock mating time. When the shooting season is at its height and we are walking home after a day in the woods, they often recall their dances with something like astonishment and assure me that they went there simply for want of a better pastime.

"Look, boys," I said, "the spring of light is in full swing. We'll have a cellarful of water soon if we're not careful. So hurry up and start shovelling."

We went for it in good earnest, and this work made us tingle with health and vigour.

I stood there leaning on the spade thrust deep in the snow, my heart brimming with love—for whom, I could not tell.

Two crows were somersaulting over the purple forest.

Why, that's whom I loved so dearly—those birds. On a bleak winter day when the frost is so severe that the sun seems crucified on dazzling pillars, and everything is buried under the snow, when man and beast have hidden away and most birds fall dead on the wing, when I am trudging along, uncertain whether I shall ever get home, it is that bird, the crow, alone that keeps me company, flying high over the desolate whiteness, its frost-bitten wing scraping the wind.

And now the carrion crows are in a love frenzy. The bird below hurtles itself against the one above it and then climbs up, then the other does the same thing, and so they keep racing, going higher and higher until suddenly they both swoop down with a cry and start it all over again.

Crows turning somersaults—what a happy sight! A melody rings in my heart—a song without words about the blue of the skies with a warm cloud, like a great white bird with a swan-like breast, unsullied and unruffled, floating across the spring-flooded spaces.

Land!

There had been no frost for three days, and the thick mist had secretly done its work on the snow.

"Come out here, Dad!" Petya called. "Listen to those buntings."

I went out and listened. It was good to hear their singing, and the breeze was soft and warm. The road had grown all rusty and hump-backed.

It was as though somebody had been trying hard to catch up with the spring and had at last succeeded and touched her, arresting her progress and making her pause for thought. The cocks were crowing all around us and the woods loomed blue in the mist.

Petya stood peering into the milky wisps and suddenly noticed something dark way off in the field.

"Look, the ground's showing!"

He ran into the house, and I heard him shouting:

"Come and have a look, Lyova! Quick—the ground is showing!"

Even Mother came out and, shielding her eyes, asked:

"Where?"

Petya ran a few steps and stood pointing at the snowy distance like Columbus.

"Land!"

The Mist

Towards noon the mist overhead thinned out in patches, and the blue of the woods deepened until they were almost violet. It was Lyova who brought the glad tidings:

"The water is rising in the hollows!" He had noticed, too, that the blackcock were settling on the trees preparing for their mating songs.

"Perhaps they're just feeding," I said.

"No," he replied, "they were perched too low—there's nothing there for them to feed on."

I walked down to the village for provisions along the high road; parallel to it ran a road which the peasants used in winter driving their sledges to market. The high road had been thawing rapidly, the water flowing down into the ditch, but the snow in the winter road, strewn with dung and pressed firm by the runners, was hard as iron; and for a long time yet the horses would be pulling the sledges to market here because this was the only passable road left.

The mist had not yet cleared away completely and the village was invisible, but I could hear the cocks crowing there. The nearer I came, the louder the crowing until it was more like a roar—the whole village seemed to be crowing like one giant cock. Soon the rooks would be calling as loudly as they fought to drive the crows out of their nests; next would come the turn of the crows, towards St. George's day, and lastly, the peasant girls would start bawling their songs.

The First Song of the Waters

Towards evening we went out to see if the hazel-grouse would respond to a decoy whistle.

In the spring it is amusing to watch them running over the hard snow, stopping now and then to listen, and often coming so close that we could almost reach out for them.

The road back was hard going because a light evening frost had crusted the snow and our feet kept breaking through and sinking. The orange sunset was hard and glassy, and the pools in the swamps glowed like window-panes. We were anxious to know whether the sound we heard was really the blackcock starting their mating songs. All three of us climbed a hillock almost free from snow and stood listening.

I puffed at my pipe—there was a light breeze from the north. We listened to windward and suddenly it dawned upon us that it was the water gurgling against the little bridge down below, very near—quite like a singing blackcock.

The Mating of the Blackcock

Stars spangled the sky. It grew colder indoors. I went out to see what it was like outside and met my neighbour, an old peasant, who had come out for an airing.

"It's freezing," I said.

He did not reply at once but looked around—at the snow and the stars—prodded the ground with his foot and said:

"The grandson has come to fetch his grandfather." *

I walked over the snow—the crust held.

"Good for the grandson," I said, and went indoors to wake up the boys.

That was probably the last hard crust that year, I told them. We ought to go to Vorogosh and see if the mating had begun. Even if

---

* That is, grandfather frost.

we didn't hear the song, we would see the traces left by the birds' wings on the snow.

"You do know your business, Dad," Lyova said happily, shaking Petya awake.

The snow was frozen hard and powdered by the latest fall. The going was pure joy, whichever way we turned. The woods and marshes for versts around were familiar and dear to us: we had beaten them for game and coursed them with hounds, and given our names to all the islands, hollows, and hillocks. We had our own Yasnaya Polyana* with three tall pines in it under which ran the hare's thoroughfare; there was a dry spot between two vast marshes that we called "Repose," and there was a "Golden Meadow" too. About eight versts further on there was a hill overgrown with pines and surrounded with swamps almost impassable at times; the local people called it simply the "Tuft," but we dubbed it the Alaun Plateau.** We easily covered the eight versts to the Tuft over the hard, powdered crust. When we had climbed the hill we caught the first breeze from the south. Then I remembered what everybody had been saying about this spring: "It will come all at once," and I began to worry—if this south wind persisted and we had a sunny day it would be a hard job to get back across the marshes.

We stood leaning against the trees waiting for the first streak of dawn and listening. It's true enough that you can spend all your life in the woods observing and studying things, yet something is always liable to happen that will stump you completely. As we stood listening we heard a crashing noise in the swamp below: the ice was breaking like shattered glass and the splinters tinkled as they fell—some huge creature was coming swiftly towards us. With our fingers on the trigger, we stood, all three of us, holding our breath, waiting for whatever would appear out of the dark. But just before it reached our island it turned off into the marshes. The crashing ceased for a time in the dry patch we called "Repose," but then began again and we could hear it for a long time and we fancied there was no end to it.

Petya was the first to catch the long-awaited whirr to the east where red dawn was breaking. Then Lyova heard it too. It must have been very far away for I couldn't hear it, but then my ears were full of a

---

* Tolstoi's famous estate is called Yasnaya Polyana ("Serene Meadow").
** Another name for Valdai Hills, a plateau in European Russia.

noise that was like the chirping of crickets and I imagined I could still hear the elk crashing through the glass in the swamp. Since they were the first to hear it, it was their job to run downhill and across the glassy swamp, taking the risk of flushing the blackcock by the sound of the breaking ice.

I was content with watching the beautiful dawn and feeling the gentle breeze on my cheek. I stood on the hill looking down on the marshes and the dark greying pines that stood here and there.

How long I had stood there I cannot say. I watched the crimson dawn for a century, it seemed, before I heard a shot down below. I was glad—gladder than if I had bagged the bird myself: somehow I am more anxious for their success than my own. But at last I had my chance too. I had taken three leaps downhill when I heard that indescribable whirr of great wings, turned quickly, saw the black shape against the red glare between the tree-tops, and fired almost point-blank. The other bird, the one I had heard in the first place, escaped. Never mind, one was good enough. The bird fell on a huge yet unthawed ant-hill under the pines, and I sat down on it with my face to the sun.

There was another shot from the same direction but I scarcely noticed it for the rising sun disclosed a world of puzzles round my ant-hill and I was trying to unravel them. There was a narrow channel of running water under the ice. It intrigued me, but I solved that one easily: when the snow had begun to thaw a field-mouse had made a groove stamping down the snow in its path. Then came another frost, and another thaw; the snow all around was quicker to melt than the compact layer in the groove, and when it froze once again the water had crept in and now ran in this channel under the ice.

Perhaps I fell asleep, but in the open I always sleep with my feelings and thoughts unbroken, oblivious only of the passage of time. I was startled awake as a twig which had been weighed down with snow so that its tip had frozen in the same spot of ice under which the mouse had made its channel, now suddenly freed itself, swung upright and stood before me, a young tree. I sat up with a start, and the sight that met my gaze was blue water, nothing but blue water around the spot we called the Alaun Plateau.

It did not even occur to me that we were cut off on our island. It didn't matter then—we would get out somehow. I was immeasurably happy to see the spring of light and water once more and I instantly remembered the words from the Good Book: "Till your land for six years and in the seventh let it rest. After seven times seven it will be your fiftieth year. Then take your trumpet and blow, for this is your jubilee."

I took the barrel off my gun and blew down the muzzle with all my might. The boys came running in alarm. I told them to do as I had done and said:

"Blow your trumpets, sons. This is my jubilee."

The Spring of Waters

Since my land is resting this year I shall write no fiction but put everything down without changing the names even, and record each day of spring: let the earth itself be the hero of my story.

I felt the urge to observe nature and put everything down when I stopped going on my long spring trips: nature came into motion when I came to a standstill. I have procured a scientific programme for nature study this year, but shall also record personal events, stray thoughts and meetings with people so that my life shall be centred about nature.

The day I put down: "The pairing of the long-tailed tits," Petya was told that their school would be reorganized into a seven-year school and he would receive his graduation certificate that year. We would have to move to another town if he wanted to go on to a secondary school. We had just been thinking that we would like to move somewhere closer to water, and had written to make inquiries in Pereslavl-Zalessky, a town on the lovely Pleshcheyevo Lake. And it so happened that on that day of the long-tailed tits and the news about Petya's school I received an answer to my letter from the director of the Pereslavl museum. He wrote that the local school was not a bad one and that the boys would be able to go on with their nature studies at the museum; there were plenty of birds around, and elk, lynx and bears in the woods; three versts from town there was an historical estate on the higher shore of the lake where the famous galley of Peter I was preserved; they were thinking of setting up a natural research station in the empty palace there, and if I cared to do some trail blazing with my nature studies I could take up any apartment in it I liked.

He then went on to tell me how we could get there; we could either take a short cut by horse and waggon or else go via Moscow by rail as far as Berendeyevo station.

I invariably succumb to the spell of such wonderfully sounding names: I imagined it was Tsar Berendei's* palace, and the more I thought about it the more excited I grew.

"Well, Berendei," I said to myself, "this is just the thing for you."

My love for nature has never prevented me from liking beautiful cities and their complex and fascinating world. But when I tire of city life I take a tram and within twenty minutes am out in the open again. I must have been cut for a free existence. I can live for years in the huts of fishermen, hunters and peasants. I get on well with working people whereas middle-class prosperity chills me and makes me feel ill at ease. This, however, does not dampen my fondness for some palaces and great cities. It's a damnable place, this hut of mine, where nothing but the oven remains dry in the heavy summer rain and where one cannot ever shed one's sheepskins in winter.

Strike while the iron's hot, hammer up the boxes and tighten the ropes and straps!

"Press it with your knee, Lyova," I shouted. "Press it down or it will come apart on the road. Oil and clean the guns, Petya. We'll be hunting lynx and bears, you know."

The boys were to stay behind until after their exams, while we went straight off. The wild geese, too, flew north, probably heading for Pleshcheyevo Lake just as we were.

The Coming of the Cranes

At last we found ourselves inside the Goritsk Monastery, lying crosswise on the Trubezh River and Lake Pleshcheyevo, with grounds large enough to shelter thousands of people. There was a time perhaps when people took refuge here from invaders. Now the place looked desolate, some of the bells were tongueless, and only a couple of goats, the property of the local historian and director of the museum, were wandering around the archbishop's fish-pond which measured exactly the size of Noah's Ark, and little Galya, the daughter of the botanist and director's assistant, was running about with them.

The smaller belfry afforded a bird's eye view of the life outside the walls—the many churches and monasteries of the ancient town and the stream of villagers winding between them, bound for the

---

* Tsar Berendei, the legendary figure of Russian folk tales, is associated with ancient national traditions and the poetry of pre-Christian beliefs.

market. Everything had got mixed up in this museum of a town: the old nunnery was still called the Blessed Virgin-on-the-Mount while the land itself bore the name of Mangy Hill and a street in it Whistling Street, re-named Voladarsky Street, and the street nearby—Falcon Lane, because the falconers of Ivan the Terrible had once lived there. And there was a forest of churches below—leaving just enough room to drive through. One of them—the Forty Martyrs'—stood where the Trubezh emptied into the lake and was dedicated to the memory of forty Christians who were drowned in some other lake somewhere. Another, on the opposite side of the estuary, was known as the Annunciation,* which meant, as the fishermen explained to me, that it served as an introduction for the famous Pereslavl herring fishery. Further on there was another sanctuary—Saint Fyodor-on-the-Hill.

It was strange to us, after celebrating the spring of the waters in the marshy land streaked with rivers, to see Lake Pleshcheyevo still lying like a snow-covered plain; one could only tell by the thin jagged fringe around it that it was a frozen lake.

On a hill to the left of the monastery stood the white palace commemorating Peter the Great and the birth of the Russian navy. On the opposite side of the lake there was another hill with an ancient monastery buried inside it, called Alexander's Hill in honour of Alexander Nevsky, the prince of Pereslavl, though the local people called it simply Yarilo's Patch.**

I learned all this as soon as I arrived from the local historian who had devoted his entire life to the study of his native Pereslavl.

"I'm the seventh tenant here," he told me in his broad Vladimir dialect. "The first was the Fool. Hence you have the Fool's Coppice, the Fool's Ravine and even one of the towers is called the Fool's Tower."

The Fool first, then the Finnish pagan priest, someone or other next, and finally the archbishop. I was impressed by the Fool and kept thinking about him while the historian told me of a certain village called Resurrection Village nicknamed the Devil's Village by the peasants.

Perhaps originally it was the Fool's Village, but in the struggle with the boisterous Fool or Yarilo, the holy fathers preached the miracle of the Resurrection until the domestic good-natured Yarilo was transformed into a mystic malicious Devil.

---

* The literary meaning of the Russian word is "introduction."
** Yarilo—the heathen god of sun and fertility among the Slavs.

All the monasteries and churches were the treasures of the museum including the galley of Peter the Great and Yarilo's Patch.

"It's quite a museum!" I said. "From Yarilo to Peter I."

"And after Peter I too," said the historian. "I could show you round the buildings of Catherine's and Elizabeth's time."

Some visitors had just arrived and we joined them in the Church of the Assumption.

He was a good host, this historian, and a real connoisseur of local lore. Moreover, true Russian that he was, he could both present the broadest outline or, if need be, take you along the narrowest of paths.

As he noticed that not all his listeners were interested in the icons of Catherine's time or in the Elizabethan baroque but were letting their eyes wander over the blue vaults, he switched on to the story about Archbishop Gennady Krotinsky who died of cholera here and was buried in the church. A grating fenced off the exact spot on the floor, and there was a hump in the centre covered with a pall. The monks used to take some sand from under the pall and distribute it among the believers who thought the sand had forced its way through the wood and the stone. Anyone could draw the pall aside now and see that the sand had been simply poured into an ordinary sugar-plum tin which actually bore the inscription "Ainem Assortment."

This failed to amuse one of the visitors though, who had shown no interest in baroque either. Mikhail Ivanovich then fell back on a fresco showing Lazarus and the Rich Man.

"Look," he said to the morose young man, "the bourgeois is boiling in hell fire while the proletarian has been taken to Abraham's bosom."

Whereupon the visitor brightened and said, "You see how long this has been going on!"

"Yes," replied the historian, "it really was very long ago."

When we came out and looked down at the lake from the monastery rampart we noticed that on this very warm day the ice had become fringed with a thin blue strip along the shore, and cranes were squawking high overhead.

The Coming of the Kestrels

Butterflies were fluttering about the sunlit courtyard of the museum. Sergei Sergeyevich, the botanist, recorded an important event that day: some tiny beetles, museum pests, had crawled over the walls into the yard. He collected some dry leaves in a bag, sifted them out, and through a magnifying glass watched the tiny crumbs come to life.

"Sergei Sergeyevich," I said, "I'm sure that you must have a favourite beetle among the sixty thousand you have collected, the one that began it all." I had to repeat my question as he did not seem to understand. "Have you got a favourite beetle?"

He reflected.

"I mean your own personal one, you know," I said uncertainly.

"Yes," he brightened up. "Only it's not one beetle but a species."

A species! The reason I had asked the question was precisely to get him away from the species and make him remember the one individual beetle which may have once flashed for him in the depths of his despair and given him a new interest in life. Well, let it be a whole species.

I asked him to name it.

The botanist, corpulent, hairy and himself like a huge beetle, beamed and answered:

"*Cetonia aurata*!"

We went into his study and inspected *Cetonia aurata*—thousands of them in glass cases or simply kept in cotton, and each one with its identification card.

As I listened to him I wanted terribly to ask him about his very first beetle and learn all those minutest personal circumstances that had led Sergei Sergeyevich into mounting *Cetonia aurata* on pins.

I have always dreamed of finding some scientific beetle that would keep me busy to the end of my days. Several times I thought I had found it, but I drained the nectar all too soon, and could not go on after that. Specializing was not for me, it seemed, unless one considered keen observation of life's phenomena a specialty.

In about an hour I had extracted all the nectar I could from Sergei Sergeyevich's collection and my attention again wandered in search of something new. I looked up and noticed that some kestrels were hovering in the sky and the blue fringe around the lake had grown wider.

I was told that if the weather kept, the pike-fishing in the lake would begin in a week or so. I decided to lose no time and call the museum committee together to tell them about my idea of organizing nature studies.

I had had some experience in this field; there was also some semblance of a method shaping in my mind. Essentially it boiled down to asserting the right of the inborn sense of one's native soil, that combines a keen feeling for nature and probably something like artistic synthesis, to be used alongside the conventional scientific methods of study. I believed that a gifted though uneducated naturalist was worth at least one or even two trained scientists.

When I had talked about it with certain outstanding scientists it always turned out that these men of genius worked just as we poor laymen did, but when I repeated the same thing to average specialists they regarded me with condescension and listened with half an ear. Perhaps I did not know how to make my ideas sound convincing? That was why this time I confined myself to a short report on our Young Naturalists club in Sokolniki Park, Moscow, and suggested that a similar organization should be set up in Pereslavl.

"The only difference is that we have comparatively little material to work on in Sokolniki and so our studies there may be described as 'micro studies' because we have a micro climate and a micro reservation, and our best work was devoted to the mosquito. Here on the other hand we can go into 'macro studies'—we can have an enormous lake and boundless forests under observation. It would be a good idea to set up a biological station with a geographical section and co-operate with Sokolniki, doing the 'macro' work ourselves and letting them go on with their 'micro studies.'"

Sergei Sergeyevich looked worried, he seemed to have interpreted my words to mean that I was anxious to avoid the dull painstaking humdrum work which in his opinion was really what shaped youngsters.

That was not at all what I had meant, but I was ready to take up the issue, arguing that the best thing for the youngsters was not the micro work in itself but kindling their enthusiasm which would make any dreary task a pleasure.

Opinion was divided: the historian and I came out for the "macro" method and we were seconded by the district committee member, while Sergei Sergeyevich won over the chairman of the Education Department. The meteorologist, a thin, sickly-looking fellow, could not make up his mind.

Before the debate was closed and the vote taken I remarked, "Though the same laws apply to a cup of tea and Lake Pleshcheyevo, a storm in a teacup would not be the same as a storm on the lake."

At this point Sergei Sergeyevich, probably wishing to take exception, jerked his arm and upset his cup of hot tea into the meteorologist's lap. The man jumped up and rushed out of the room.

"Are you all right?" we asked anxiously when he returned.

"Yes," he replied coolly. "You may be macro or micro but I am just wet." *

The committee decided that: 1. a representative from Sokolniki be invited during the holidays, to help specify the aims of our club, 2. the newly-arrived phenologist be accommodated in a four-room flat on the south side of the palace at Botik.

The Passage of the Swans

The sky had been clear since dawn, the morning frost soon melted, and towards midday an overcoat became a nuisance. The gulls had come before me and were now screaming over the weedy monastery ponds.

I walked along the shore of the lake to get to my new lodgings at Botik. One shore, the older one, was higher, cut with ravines and streams, while the other one was low and marshy. The ravines were known by the old Slavonic word *vrag*. The one nearest the monastery was known as Fool's Vrag; then came a narrow river which ran past Veskovo village and Memeka Hill, and further on, Assumption Vrag and Princeling Hill, and finally Gremyachy ("Roaring") Hill with its Gremyachy Spring. It was on this hill that the galley of Peter the Great or *botik* was preserved like a sacred relic and gave the whole estate the name of Botik.

No sooner had I climbed Gremyachy Hill and taken a look round than Nadezhda Pavlovna, the caretaker's wife, told me a story about Tsar Peter. He was a great lover of water, and one day, catching sight of Lake Pleshcheyevo, he turned his horse and dashed straight through the ripe corn towards it. A woman, reaping rye near the village of Veskovo, saw the rider wading through the cornfield and began to abuse him in no uncertain terms. Vastly amused, Peter freely rewarded the villagers and even summoned one or two of them to sit on his council, or "Duma." That was how the surname Dumnov originated in the village. Ivan Akimovich, the caretaker, was also a Dumnov, which meant that one of his forebears must have sat on Peter's Duma.

I was shown around the shed housing the *botik* with the bottom

---

* A play on words in Russian—wet is "mokro."

rotten through, the sole relic of Peter's fleet "built for the amusement of the young Tsar." I remembered that Peter re-visited the place after a space of thirty years and, indignant at the way his fleet had been left to rot, issued a harsh ukase to the governors of Pereslavl. This naturally prompted the governors to action at first, but then they again let things drift until only one galley remained, a hulk which passed from one owner of the estate to the next. Tsar Nicholas I finally made the local gentry buy the boat. They also built a small palace at the spot with a triumphal arch and a monument of marble bearing an inscription taken from Peter's ukase.

"You, the governors of Pereslavl, shall preserve the remnants of these ships, yachts and galleys, and should you neglect this obligation, you and your descendants will stand to answer for contempt of this ukase."

I was impressed by Peter's words and walked to the edge of the hill to look at the lake and visualize it as the cradle of the Russian fleet. The fringe of water along the shore had grown more defined by the end of the day and looked crimson beneath the great disc of the setting sun. My ear caught those subtle and melodious sounds which told me that the swans were flying far above.

In the palace we found some trestles and boards out of which we made beds and tables. We gave the whole place a thorough cleaning and sat listening to the grunting of a tree in the forest—something which can usually be heard only in the darkest and deepest ravines —and we were in a palace with great tall windows! We were sorry we could not find a hole in the stove in which to plant the chimney of our samovar and had to take it out on the porch to kindle. But as I went out there to do it I heard the mating-cry of the blackcock within a hundred paces of the doorway. And when I went down into the cellar for some kindling, out jumped a huge grey hare and scampered off.

We drank our tea listening with delight to the deep grunting of the tree.

The Flowering of the Nut-Tree

The woods were a mottled patchwork of dark and white, the water gurgled in the ravines, and higher up, warmed by the sun, the nut-tree burst into its golden catkins. Yarik made his first point by ear, mistaking the gurgling water for the cry of the blackcock. The real blackcock was crying some distance away, and, when we flushed him, four hens flew up with him. Our tree went on grunting, we could hear it by day and at night too through the tightly shut windows. I came to love it, it was a kindred soul; though I don't speak about it much I, too, feel like grunting with pleasure in spring.

The edge of the lake opposite Botik was still frozen but the pike could come up and reach the shore through the tunnels in the ice. Our caretaker Dumnov took up his post with his fish-spear—a veritable Neptune; further on stood the two famous pike-fishers, the brothers Komisarov, then the sacristan, and so on along the shore up to Nadgorod on our side and up to Zaozerye on the other—Neptunes all round.

I was told that the pike came up between the first light of dawn and sunrise, about nine in the morning, at noon, and then again from five till sunset. I told the Neptunes that when the lake at Tsaritsino was dragged they caught a pike that tipped the scale at three poods and had a golden ring on it put on by Boris Godunov. I wondered if there could be a pike like that in Pleshcheyevo.

"Yes," they said, "but the lake is very deep and a pike like that never comes up. Still, there is an ide in there that was ringed by Peter I."

"Has anybody caught a pike lately?"

"They haven't come out yet but we do get plenty of 'milkers.' "

They called "milkers" the male pike, much smaller than the female.

The miller came to ask me to join him in his duck shooting with a decoy. Somehow I couldn't believe his duck would be a good decoy and so I refused. He was covered with mud from head to foot and I remarked that it was unseemly for a former nobleman to go about in such a state.

"It can't be helped, you know," he muttered.

"But why is your helpmate so neat and clean?" I said, indicating his companion.

The young man explained in guilty embarrassment that he had been to the district executive committee that day and on such occasions he never bothered to wash and sometimes even made himself dirty on purpose: nowadays one had to look like a worker if one wanted to get on, he said.

Towards evening it looked like rain.

As the windows had single frames and the trees were so close, it was like sleeping in a forest. My dreams reflected the outside world like a mirror. The grunting tree dominated them all—I saw myself standing in a deep ravine like that tree. Then the sharp call of a duck pierced the fabric of my dreams and I realized that this must be the miller's decoy. Then I heard her frantic "ah, ah" which meant that she had seen the drake. I jumped out of bed and rushed for the front door, but the drake must have been swimming towards the duck in the meantime, for when I opened the door I heard a shot. In the half-light I could not see the duck, only the miller's hut.

The miller shot two more drakes while I waited for the samovar to boil.

After breakfast, when I thought the duck shooting must be over, I walked down to the mill. As soon as I saw the miller's home I nicknamed him Robinson, for there was an air of shipwreck about it: everything was broken, dirty and scattered about in the hut, and the sky peeped in through the holes in the roof. Robinson himself sat by a glowing stove plucking a duck, while his shooting companions sat by his side peeling potatoes. The most prominent among them was Yozhka; he was telling them about the blackcock: some were bluish and others yellowish; snipe also varied in size; and as for the mallard they were all so different that you could always tell one from another just like human beings; that went for hares, too.

Who were these men? Some petty clerks and mechanics who were regarded as half-savages in the town. Yet they were true students of nature, and a real feeling for nature—neither born of urban sentimentality nor of reading too much Rousseau or Tolstoi—lingered in them and them alone. It was their sort that would make the best helpmates in my studies of wildlife. I told them what was on my mind, and we agreed, then and there, not to shoot any nesting birds around Botik, nor hares if we could help it.

Speaking of hares, I told them that I had surprised one in my cellar at Botik.

"A grey hare?" asked Yozhka. "There are always hares in Botik in the winter and even in Pereslavl itself. Do you know K.'s house? No? And M.'s? Whose house do you know then?"

I told him that I knew the ancient buildings of the town: the twelfth-century cathedral, the ruins of the watermill and the fortress, the potteries where the Danilov Monastery stood now and the Tokhtamish pillar.

"So you know the Tokhtamish pillar? Well, just opposite there is a cottage with a large vegetable garden. A hare lived there, feeding on the cabbage stumps. With the first snow we set the dogs on its trail."

Yozhka gave us a full account of the chase through various historical places: out of the town to the Botik, across the lake to the famous Alexandrov Hill where they had made excavations and found a pagan Slavonic temple; then back to the town again along Soviet Street and through the fortress where the hare struck its right eye against an iron rod and, to escape the pursuit of some boys, dashed into the open doors of the militia station. Having lost its trail some time before, the men whistled to their dogs, put them on the leash and were walking back home, when they suddenly came upon the fresh tracks on Soviet Street and unleashed the dogs again. The trail led them straight into the militia station and the entire pack in full cry tore into the office, with their masters bringing up the rear. By this time the militia men had caught the hare and were already drawing lots as to who would get it.

When I got home I put the story down. I had never chased a hare through a town, and I thought its flight through many historical places most curious. I had got as far as the hare putting its eye out when my memory failed me, and I had to go down to the miller's cottage again. Robinson was alone.

"Do you remember where the hare struck his right eye against a rod?"

"In the square in front of the Church of the Holy Ghost," Robinson replied. "There's an iron railing there."

Time and Love

The mother of my decoy had been a plain domestic duck. But her father had been a wild drake, and the ducklings were the living image of their father. I picked out the one with the loudest voice and used her to attract the drakes. No end of suitors in their nuptial attire were enticed to their doom by her beguiling quacking. A sportsman is usually merciless; yet on one occasion, I hadn't the heart to shoot.

Twilight was falling when I went out into the woods, took my decoy out of her basket and, tying a long string to her leg with a weight at the end, set her on the shallow waters, while I took cover in my hut of rushes where I could watch her through a slit in the wall.

A mallard couple was flying over: the grey duck in the lead with the drake following in his courting attire. Suddenly another couple appeared from the opposite direction. Just as the two were about to meet a hawk swooped down on the duck of the second pair but missed. The duck came down and hid in a thicket. Nonplussed, the hawk slowly rose into the bluish cloud above. Recovering from the shock, the drake who was left alone made a narrow circle, but nowhere could he see his duck. Some distance away, the first pair were continuing their flight. The lone drake must have thought that this was his own duck being pursued by a stranger, and set off to overtake them.

The lost duck soon got over her fright, swam out of the thicket and began to call. As another drake came over, a contest of voices began between my decoy and her wild rival; though my duck nearly burst with her cries she was outcalled by the wild bird who got the drake.

After making a wide circle, the first pair returned still pursued by the disconsolate drake. Could he still be thinking that it was his own duck pursued by a stranger?

Meanwhile, his own duck was preening herself contentedly and silently. And my decoy, unrivalled, tried to vamp the drake and succeeded. I wonder if it's true that in their love it does not matter which duck it is as long as it is a duck. Perhaps time went so much faster for them that a few moments of separation seemed equal to ten years of our unrequited passion? Perhaps in his hopeless pursuit of his imaginary mate, the sound of the real duck's stirring voice brought back the image of his beloved so vividly that he fell in love with the whole of the river and woods?

He swooped down at my decoy so swiftly that I had no chance to shoot. Afterwards he made the drake's customary circle of gratification, floating round her. I could have shot him easily but I remembered my own youth when I was in love with the whole world and let him go.

The Sap Rises in the Birches

I cut myself a thin birch twig to clean my pipe with. A drop of sap gathered in the cut and sparkled in the sunlight. The forest was all patches: a patch of snow here, a patch of bluish water there. It was very warm by day. It seemed to me that the mating flight of the snipe might begin at any time, and in the afternoon I went to Solomidino to ask Mikhail Ivanovich Mineyev, an old wildfowler, to show me the best place for stand-shooting. He did not look like a very old man though he remembered Tsar Alexander II well, and though his grandson had just become father to a little boy. The old man was difficult to locate: he had four sons but no home of his own and moved from one son to the next like a rustic King Lear. He had already quarrelled with two of them irrevocably and was now staying with his third.

People told me all about it while they helped me track him down, and later, as we waited for nightfall in his cottage, the old man told me a great deal more about himself. He went on with talking as we walked to the place of the stand-shooting but I had given up listening by then and was anxious to get rid of him. I couldn't help hearing his words, though, and I answered at random, just to say something.

"Then the court says to give him the cow."

"Did it?"

"So help me: the cow."

The old man had got hold of my sleeve, blocking the way, ruining the silence and shutting out the whole world. He wanted my opinion. Bother the man! My tongue answered of its own accord.

"Just think of it."

He let go of my sleeve, stepped forward and said:

"Then I dropped my son the way I dropped your sleeve just now and went on to the next one."

I heard the "swees-swees" of a duck overhead but the old man's chatter gave me no chance to take aim.

"They've got the samovar going at your place, you know. You'll be late for your tea."

"That's right," he said. "But I don't drink tea, what's tea! They've got a log that wants shifting."

"Why don't you go then?"

"It's a great big log!"

He laughed and walked off, but, overcome again, he turned, repeating:

"A walloping big log!"

It occurred to me that while the sons shouldered all the cares and work of the season the old man had the time to go shooting, enjoy the re-awakening of nature and chatting with a new arrival.

"You're a sly old fellow," I said.

He seemed very pleased, walked back to me again and winked cheerfully.

"It's true enough, it's they who pay the taxes and insurance and everything, not I. . . ."

This time I didn't let the chance slip and fired without taking aim at the second of the two birds flying swiftly overhead. It turned out to be a large drake chasing a duck. He rustled down through a birch and fell on a virgin patch of snow below.

"Go on with you," I said to the old man. "Be off and have your tea."

"I will, too, I'll have my tea and go shooting when I like, but with them it's nothing but taxes and insurance all the time."

Contrary to all my expectations and former experience the silence which resumed after the old man left me was not the deep silence, tense with the power of new life: the silence was dead. The only sounds in the whole forest were a lonely thrush singing its dismal song, and the sparkling birch sap dripping from a cut. This silence unnerved me, the harmony was broken, and the forest seemed to me as terrifying as to a superstitious man who imagines all sorts of horrors. It was terrifying to me because I lost my sense of balance and felt like shouting and shooting into the trees or at anything else in my way. Suddenly I heard the shouts of men approaching through a clearing and as they came nearer I recognized the voices of Robinson and Yozhka, and guessed that the party was returning from their stand-shooting.

"What's the row about?" I asked when they came up.

"I was just saying that it was all lies that Robinson told you this morning," said Yozhka.

"No, it wasn't," said Robinson. "The hare could have easily struck his eye on the railings round the Church of the Holy Ghost."

"But you never saw it! Those bars are finger thick. He simply plucked his eye out on the barbed wire."

Their opinion on the woodcock was divided: some said it was too early; others, that they had come but the mornings were too cold for them to fly for pairing; still others claimed that they had died of cold in the south and there wouldn't be any stand-shooting at all.

"Has the pairing of the snipe begun?" I asked.

"The snipe are here."

"Have you heard the curlew?"

"They're whistling all right."

"It's odd that the woodcock have not come."

"Most likely they've all died of cold."

The Old Pike

I was returning from town very late that evening. I usually got a lift from the timber cartmen on their way home; and sure enough, a young cartman, who had evidently taken a glass or two after his hard day's work, offered me a lift. I refused at first as custom demanded it but when he asked me again I got into the sledge. He said he was Ivan Bazunov from Veslev.

"The famous pike-fisher?" I asked.

"An expert of sorts," he replied. "May I ask your name?"

I told him.

"Well, Mikhail Mikhailovich," he said. "Have you got a pet affliction?"

"A chronic one, my dear Bazunov. Haven't you heard that I was a huntsman?"

"So it's you. Of course, I've heard of you. Very pleased to meet you. A huntsman, to be sure? Well, and I go for pike. I know all the ins and outs of it. That's been my university, all right. Have I got the word right?"

"Quite."

"Good for me! I'll explain it all now. I'm a pike-fisher and that's my pet affliction. I go for pike, of course, but take human beings. For instance a chap would like to make love to his sweetheart in broad daylight but it's out of the question with people all around—just isn't done. Did you ever have to go through this, Mikhail Mikhailovich?"

"Who didn't," I said.

"Then you agree about human beings. Now let me tell you that it's just the same with other living creatures—pike, too. Its roe begins to swell but it simply can't be done. Just as there's the night for human beings there's its own lawful time for the pike."

"I know," I said. "During the first thaw."

"That's right. When the first water flows into the lake, the she-pike goes upstream and then I throw up everything and go to the lake."

Bazunov then told me at great length how he fought and coaxed his wife to let him go. At the turning to my house he detained me, insisting that I hear his story to the end.

"When the sun gets warmer humans go keen on marriage, and it's the same with the pike, because the roe gets the better of her. She presses against the bottom of a shallow place to squeeze the roe out of herself, and the milkers whiten it over. I've seen as many as seven at a time swishing over a large old pike, and those who don't know, will strike a milker while the pike herself, the largest of the lot, gets away. But I know what's what and plunge my spear well below the milkers because I am an expert of sorts."

I also told him a story which puzzled me: one evening in July I had been walking by the shore and noticed what appeared to be a man's hand popping out of the water. It looked very much as if the waves had washed a corpse ashore. As I came nearer I saw that it was not a man's hand but a large pike. I shot it, but the meat was very tough—it was too old.

"Now you've been saying," I concluded, "that the pike knows her proper time like a human being and comes to the shore in early spring. But this was in the middle of summer. What do you think of that?"

"I'll tell you," said Bazunov. "On a warm sunny day the pike is sometimes drawn to the shore. She too has her memories just like a human being. You can believe me because I'm an expert of sorts. An old woman will play the fool worse than a young one sometimes because she can't rid herself of her memories of love."

Pike-Fishing

There was a spell of warm, almost hot days and moonlit nights with such heavy frosts that the fringe of water along the lake froze an inch deep by morning. This fringe was like a wide blue river now and the ice only held fast in the inlets. But on market days the peasants still drove their sledges across the lake from Usolye to Pereslavl.

The pike-fishing had begun; only the mornings were wasted because the water froze overnight and even if a pike came up it was impossible to get near it soundlessly. The pike-fishers, however, would take up their positions at regular intervals and stand stock-still with their spears raised to strike. In the evenings there were lights all along the water's edge. They waded in threes knee-deep between the ice and the shore, one carrying a torch, and the other two their raised spears. The largest pike might appear at any hour now.

I tried to come up and talk to the men but they obviously disliked it and moved away whenever they saw anyone coming. Then I took up a position with my gun but found it unbearably dull. I could not understand how they had the patience. But finally I did understand: when one of them saw a fish and stole up to it with a raised spear the others watched him tensely—it was not the hope of gain that whetted their interest but the thrill of the hunt.

When it was nearly dark and the people gathered to prepare for torch-fishing, the news of the day was carried round the lake from fisherman to fisherman.

Today's news was that a pike weighing about eighteen pounds had been caught at the mouth of the Trubezh River. The fisherman, they said, had been sitting on a beam when he spotted a huge fish and had pounced on it like a fish-hawk. He failed to kill it, merely embedding his spear in it like a fish-hawk its talons. The fish fought so hard that the man fell into the icy water, still gripping his spear. He went under but came up again near a floe and finally landed the exhausted fish.

Someone else in the town was said to have tossed a spear from the pier at a huge pike and dashed into the water after it, but the fish got away, spear and all.

Meanwhile Dumnov, the man whose forebears had sat in Peter's Duma, had noticed a huge head popping out of the water and so he hauled a beam through the shallow water some distance away from the rest of the men, and crossed over it to the solid ice.

The people ashore saw Dumnov raise his spear, but he did not strike, afraid that the pike might pull him under.

The men abused him and laughed at him, but Dumnov merely sent for a bottle of vodka, gulped it down and watched the water stolidly.

Suddenly all doubts about Dumnov's pike were dispelled: they all saw the enormous head popping from under the ice and vanishing again. Dumnov asked for another bottle and emptied it.

Just then the huge head came up once more and this time Dumnov hit well—the fish was pinned to the bottom. But what was he to do next—the end of his spear hardly showed above the water. He could not haul up a pike that size with his spear, nor could he reach it with his hands. Those two bottles of vodka stood him in good stead now: the sea is only knee-deep for a drunken man, says an old proverb. Dumnov slipped into the icy water and stood on the pike's back. Then he vanished under the water, stuck his fingers in the pike's eyes, reappeared and dragged his quarry ashore: a huge pike and a milker weighing about ten pounds for all to see.

Dumnov dumped the pike into a pit where she suddenly came to life again. What a fish! She swished her tail and off flew the ten-pound milker, landing some fifty paces away.

Dumnov roped the fish under the gills with his belt and lifted her so that her head came level with his shoulders, while the tail trailed along the ground. As he walked through the village all the men and women poured out, and word flew ahead of him: Dumnov has killed a pike he can hardly drag home.

And so the news spread round the lake from Veskovo to Nadgorod, from Nadgorod to Zaozerye and through Uryov to Usolye: Dumnov in Veskovo had killed a sixty-pound pike and a milker weighing a full ten.

The Frogs Are Astir

We took our decoy duck and spent the next night in a hide-out. There was a very severe frost towards dawn and the water was frozen; I was so chilled I felt out of sorts all day and developed a fever towards the evening. I spent the next day in bed, fighting my illness with all my concentrated efforts. At dawn on the third day I dreamed about the lacy shore of Lake Pleshcheyevo and the white gulls riding the blue water near the ice-bound inlets. It was perfectly true to life, I knew it. Those white gulls were so lovely against the blue, and so many other fine things lay in store for me: I would see the lake completely rid of ice and the earth covered with grass and the birch-trees rustling in their new garb.

Our tree had stopped grunting. I wondered why. Instead, a bird was singing.

"Could it be a finch?"

I was told that the weather had turned warmer the day before and peals of distant thunder had been heard.

Still weak after the battle with my illness but happy over my victory, I made my way to the window and saw that the meadow in front of the house was dotted with birds: finches, and all varieties of thrushes. They were hopping about the meadow, bathing in a large pool. So the singing birds had all come back!

Our dogs, tied to the trees, began to bark suddenly, looking stupidly at something on the ground.

"Look what the thunder has done," Dumnov said, pointing to the spot.

A frog, its wet back glistening in the sun, was leaping towards the dogs, but just before they could pounce upon it the frog swerved on its course and made for a large pool.

Yes, the frogs had come to life, and it did look as if the thunder had done it. The life of the frogs seemed to be influenced by thunder in some curious way. No sooner had there been a peal of thunder than the frogs were astir, hopping along in pairs, their backs shining in the sun and all making for the large pool. As I came near, they all peeped out to have a look at me: they are a terribly curious lot.

Insects were swarming in the sun, and there was a great to-do of birds in the meadow. But when I got up that day I did not want to be bothered with their names. I felt an awareness of nature as a whole and wanted no names. I felt my kinship with all those flying, swimming, running creatures, each of whom had left a memory stirring in my blood over the millions of years intervening between us: all this had once been part of me and all I had to do was to look and recognize.

My thoughts cropping up from my sense of being alive were simple: for a short time illness had separated me from life and now I had to make up for what I had lost. It is thus that millions of years ago we lost our wings which were as beautiful as those of the sea-gulls, and because it was so long ago we admire them so much now.

We lost the ability to swim like fish or swing on a bough of a mighty trunk or be carried from place to place, a flying seed, and we delight in all this because it once belonged to us, though a long, long time ago.

I was resting from my illness that day and could not work. Why not indulge myself a little in more homespun philosophy? Is it not a crude truth that man creates the world in his own image and semblance, yet the world can go on without man? The artist should feel this more keenly than anyone, and become entranced so completely that he should believe in the existence of things, dead or living, apart from himself. I think that science merely puts the finishing touch to what the artist has re-created of images forever lost. The artist, feeling his kinship with the bird, gives wings to his image—and we first fly with him in thought, when along comes the savant with his figures and we continue on mechanical wings. Art and science put together are the power that recovers our lost kinship.

Towards midday there was a distant peal of thunder just as the day before, and later came a steady warm rain. In an hour the ice on the lake turned from white to transparent, assuming the blue of the sky, like the strip of water along the shore, and at last the whole of it was one complete expanse.

After the evening glow a mist rose over the paths in the forest, and hazel-hens whirred up in pairs from under one's feet at every ten paces. The grouse clucked as loudly as they could and all the trees seemed to be muttering and hissing. Then the mating flight of the woodcock began.

There were triple lights in the darkness: the blue stars above, the yellow glare of the town on the horizon, and the red torches of the fishermen over the lake. When the red specks came nearer, we could see the smoke as well, and the people with their spears, very much like the figures with the dragons on the Olbia and Panticapaeum vases.

But I have forgotten to put down the most important thing of all: after a long search we found the grunting tree—it was a birch rubbing against an aspen in a breeze. But now the chafed spot exuded abundant sap and the tree was silent.

THE SPRING OF GREEN GRASS

The Arrival of the Finches

Between the arrival of the finches and the first call of the cuckoo, our spring appears in all its beauty as subtle and complex as the intertwining branches of a still leafless birch. During this time the snow will melt away and the waters will swell into torrents and the land will be strewn with the first and sweetest flowers, and the buds of the poplar will burst open and the fragrant sticky leaves will part, and then will come the cuckoo. And only then, having missed all the miracle of it, people will say: Spring has come. Isn't it beautiful!

To the huntsman, though, the coming of the cuckoo means that spring is over. It's no longer spring, if all the birds have nested, and their busiest time has begun.

With the arrival of the cuckoo the forests are overrun with strangers, and the casual shot of some idler jars upon your nerves so badly that you make off as fast as you can to avoid hearing another. Or you may be walking through the dew-drenched grass of a morning and suddenly you see some footprints and realize that someone was walking in front of you. Immediately you turn and walk in another direction, changing all your plans, simply because you have seen a stranger's tracks on the grass. Or you may happen to come to a secluded spot and sit down on a stump to rest for a while, thinking that the forest is so vast that there must be at least a square foot of it somewhere untrodden by man, and that perhaps no one has ever sat on this stump before. and then your eyes stray round, to discover a crushed eggshell close by.

I had often heard that a mushroom detected by a human eye ceased to grow. But I had checked it on several occasions and found it was not true: the mushroom did grow. I also heard that birds shifted their eggs if detected by man. But when I checked this I discovered that the birds were simple and trusting.

When the finches have arrived but the snow in the forest is still untouched by thaw I like to walk to some ridge and stand waiting for I know not what. It is hardly ever perfect, I must say: there will be always one nuisance or another—either a frost or drizzling rain or the wind whistling dismally through the bare branches. But at last an evening does come when the early willow bursts into leaf, there's a smell of grass, and the primroses come out. And then I remember how many evenings I have waited, how much I have been through for this one beautiful evening on earth. Then it almost seems to me that I have also taken part in its creation together with the sun, the wind and the clouds, and the answer grows clear:

"It was worth waiting for."

The Torrent

As soon as the migration of the finches began I remembered the Popov Meadow and the bushes surrounding it and went to have a look if that was perhaps where the birds were resting. I was not mistaken: the bushes were strewn with tiny birds and the air was dim with specks as if someone were casting poppyseed about with a trowel. I flushed a host of wood pigeons, and instantly a hawk got one of them. A brown owl flew by and a crow, emerging from God knows where, began fretting it. Two pairs of cranes met and flew together, soon followed by a large flock of them in a regular triangle. Some queerly shaped birds appeared from time to time, but looking through my binoculars, I usually found they were either crows or jackdaws carrying something to their nests. But there was one strange white bird I could not identify for a long time because of its immense size. Fortunately the mysterious creature was heading in my direction, and at last I saw that it was a jackdaw carrying a whole newspaper. When, blinded by its burden, it almost butted into me, I shouted and the newspaper dropped to the foot of the hill, not far away.

Soon after sunrise a heavy cloud came over and broke into a short rain, but towards midday the sun grew warmer and there was more water everywhere. The fields were patches of colour. The road, washed out in places, turned out to be a ridge of ice about four feet thick. The old man from Dyadkovo—I recognized him through my bin-oculars, the same old man whose sons had been killed in the war and who now shared a wretched hut with all their widows—was trundling along with a load of hay which he must have saved all winter to fetch the highest price. I felt for him, and watched with some anxiety, wondering what he would do when he got to the washed-out spot. It would seem that there was less water on top of the ridge while down below there was a regular swamp of slush and mud. But the old man stubbornly preferred to go straight through the mud, got stuck immediately, but soon pulled clear and drove on. A young fellow who came along just after him with another cart of hay thoughtlessly swerved to the opposite side of the road and instantly his horse sank in the slush up to the neck. Standing waist-deep in water, the young man began to unharness it, swearing violently. A crowd gathered, each offering a helping hand, the women as well as the men. They were apparently using the shaft as a lever: the women bore down on one end while the men heaved at the cart and finally set it back on the road. When the horse was harnessed again and the young fellow turned the cart homewards, someone shouted, "You can thank your stars! A man was drowned here this time last year."

I faced about and saw some blackcock flying over to Bilberry Ra-vine. I called to them and they came scurrying back across Popov Meadow as obediently as chicks. A hen-harrier flew past. A brown owl settled on a pine-tree. Wood-pigeons were feeding together in a large flock. Then they rose into the air, probably scared away by a hawk. As I turned to follow their flight, I saw the same young peasant coming back with his load of hay. I suppose he was so set on selling his hay and having a drink in town that he came back to have another try. Or perhaps someone had told him that the old man had managed to get through safely and he knew now that he should drive not along the top but down below. Confidently he followed the old man's way, got through easily and trotted on.

The torrent was rushing into the lake, filling the seams in the ice.

A fish-hawk flew past chased by some carrion crows. Then some singing thrushes appeared and somewhat apart from them, a marvellous slim black thrush, with a golden bill.

The torrent was raging in the depths of the ravine. I sat on the edge of the drop, whistling to the hazel-hens. A solitary grouse was gabbling in the slender birch-tree while a wood-pigeon cooed strenuously nearby. Never before had I seen or heard so many tiny birds. There were swarms of them: suddenly they would all fly up like a cloud of mosquitoes, frisking through the branches, coupling in the air, and spilling out into the meadow, all of them singing. And this twittering of the birds and the gurgling of the torrent and the gabbling of the grouse and the cooing of the wood-pigeons and the clamour of the cranes stirred up one's deepest thoughts.

I found a path down to the stream, cut a long pole with my hatchet and crossed the water supporting myself on it. I then left my pole in a conspicuous place, enjoying the thought that it might be of use to someone else wanting to cross the torrent.

Now I needed all my keenness for intuition alone could guide me to where the woodcock would be flying. All the meadows seemed equally attractive, but I was determined to find the best one while there was time. One meadow caught my fancy at last. On my right there was a ribbon of birch-trees rising out of the stream's swampy banks, with the dark pine forest showing behind, while on the left the dry ground rose to a small ridge covered with shrubs. I would wait for the woodcock in the little valley between the dry ridge and the swampy forest. Juniper bushes grew here and there in my meadow, with a single tall fir-tree among them, and perched on the top of it was a thrush whistling from time to time on its flute as if conducting the choir of evening forest sounds.

I was not sure that the afterglow of the sunset would last so I could wait for the dawn right under this bush. Before it grew too dark I looked about for a well-remembered path to the shack where they used to brew corn wine. Finding it I set to work making a bed of fir branches and kindling a fire. I slept so lightly that I heard my own snores and woke up instinctively whenever the fire needed tending.

I awoke when the morning frost had turned to dew and the drops were glistening in the sun. Numerous birds that you can only see for the few days of migration were singing praises to the sunshine and the already green earth. I would listen for a long moment, and then look through my splendid binoculars, focussing the singer to its tiniest feather. Throwing the reflection from prism to prism, my instrument, like an artist, created form out of chaos, and to this I added something of my own.

Later I strolled into a clearing and, watching the path through my binoculars, saw a girl walking across the fields towards the stream where I had left the pole the night before. Her orange skirt was fastened to her shoulder and in her hand she carried a pair of shiny new rubbers which she only wore to church, and an umbrella opened very rarely, only when there were people around and no danger of rain.

I was glad that my pole helped the girl to cross, but it pained me to see her hide it in the bushes afterwards and cover it with leaves.

Someone on the other side, however, must have been watching the girl, too, and she was no sooner out of sight than he found the pole, hid it elsewhere, and took cover in the bushes. It was clear the girl would soon return and so I sat on a stump, waiting for my pole to cross back again.

Swarms of finches were flying from the clearing to the green cornfields, racing in their courting flight, falling in pairs, and fluttering back to continue their singing.

At last I saw the girl in the orange skirt. She reached the stream, and finding no pole, ran about in a flurry looking for it.

I lowered my binoculars. I could see with the naked eye the satyr emerge from his bushes, produce the pole and help the girl to the other side.

The Topic

In the fishermen's village of crowded ramshackle huts I saw the gulls perched on the mooring posts, unmolested by the children who were playing close by. I remembered how hard it had been to teach my own better bred children to be kind to live things, and thought that many generations of fishermen must have come and gone to instil the precept of sparing these beautiful though probably quite useless birds so that now their children would never think of throwing stones at them; the spark of human kindness was one, whether kindled by Raphael's Madonna or by a gull as in the case of these poor fishermen.

Petya and Lyova arrived today and were thrilled with the gulls. To have a better look they ran nearer and the gulls all rose from their nests, blotting out the sky, then scattered like huge snow-flakes and

settled in the green cornfields, turning them quite white. We were
told that the gulls were protected by the local people, and that shooting them was strictly forbidden.

I was glad my boys would have nice friends: Mikhail Ivanovich's
children, Sonya and Seva, just finishing secondary school, Sergei Sergeyevich's daughter Galya, and his three student sons. As it was a
holiday, they all dressed up, drank some wine "for better friendship,"
and even danced in the courtyard of the museum.

Suddenly, like a bolt from the blue, three delegates arrived from
the Sokolniki Young Naturalists Post. One was wearing an old Aus-
trian greatcoat, the second an English one and the third that of the
Russian army. When they took them off they looked even worse: one
fellow's trousers did not even reach his boots properly. They all carried kitbags, nets and pistols in their belts. The new-comers and our
dressed-up boys and girls met like creatures of different worlds: there
was a how d'you do and nothing more. Even Lyova, the most un-
conventional of all, must have been influenced by the general festive
mood, for when he brought the new-comers to me at Botik he
announced:

"Some rum characters to see you from Sokolniki."

They gave their names. The young men had heard of me and were
very respectful. Encouraged by their sympathy, I immediately trotted
out my hobby-horse: I told them I wanted to set up a biological post
with emphasis on locality study and that I personally wished to work
on bringing science and art closer together.

"Most plants and animals are closely connected with the life of
man," I said, "but up to now science has done little to study this
relationship, and that is where art comes in. Take the gull and the
fisherman, for example, and observe how the life of these poor folk
is linked with this lovely bird."

"That's a topic," the eldest of my listeners remarked, jotting something in his notebook.

"We'll discuss it today after the meeting," muttered the other two.

"Do you discuss everything you hear?" I asked.

"Yes," answered the eldest. "We discuss everything and then act
upon our decision collectively, so that not a minute is wasted."

"So you didn't just come to have a talk with me?"

"We've come to size you up as a force."

"And what's your verdict, may I ask?"

"We find you could be very useful to us as a propagandist: you can
speak and write very well. As a scientist you are probably on the

superficial side, but as an observer you are excellent. It would also be a good thing if you took up ringing the birds because you are a huntsman and can catch a lot of them."

I shook hands with them on it, smiling, and then they told me something about themselves. The eldest was twenty. He had finished secondary school and was working as a laboratory assistant at the biological station and besides taught science at school. He was a tall young man with pleasant features, very much the leader and something of the chairman type. The second was younger, quieter, more given to reflection. He must be an efficient worker; the secretary type. The third, a sturdy-looking fellow with a sailor's tattoo on his wrist, had a curious life-story. He had been a homeless waif, but one day chance brought him to the biological post where he saw street urchins like himself working with microscopes. He had a peep too. And just as in earlier times a man would suddenly see the light and enter a monastery, so this boy was converted to science. He took up his studies enthusiastically and was now through secondary school. There was something oriental about his face, though his name was Palkin, a thoroughly Russian one.

"You understand us so well," they said. "It's not like talking to the Konsomols."

"But aren't you Konsomol members yourselves?"

"Of course. And Communists, too. We are students of nature besides, and that's why we have a deeper understanding of social phenomena."

Suddenly they all looked at the clock; they had to hurry to a meeting organized by the local Konsomols where they would propound their new method.

"Do you think we could set up a biological post here with your help?" I asked when they were leaving.

Said the chairman:

"We'll weigh up everything and then give you a definite answer."

First Shoots of Grass

The sky had been overcast since morning and there was a warm steady drizzle.

The first shoots had sprouted in the meadows and the time of spring carpets had come.

"The sheep could graze even now," I heard talk in the kitchen.

Only a few patches of snow still clung to the hollows on the northern slope of Gremyachy Hill. One could see the moles were working hard.

The sun came through the clouds at five o'clock and the air became wonderfully transparent. With the naked eye I could see Gorodishche, and Alexandrov Hill and Yarilo's Patch quite clearly. The tune of the first round dance of the season reached me from the village. A southwest breeze had driven the ice from our shore of the lake, and, yellowish in the evening glow, it seemed to touch the piles of blue clouds above.

The delegates called upon me again and asked me to lend them some guns and take them to the mating flight shoot. I gave them the guns, but unable to take them myself suggested Petya as a guide. They exchanged glances and the chairman announced he would stay behind to have a talk with me, which meant that he was sacrificing the shoot to study my possibilities as a force. I did not resent it in the least. I also liked to study people and things. I had motives of my own, and thought that two could play at that game. In my young days I was a member of an underground commune and now I had the advantage of my reminiscences.

"So there are fifteen people in your commune? Eight young men and seven girls? In other words one young naturalist is short of a girl friend."

"We don't go in for that."

"You have misunderstood me. I simply meant friendship that might lead to deeper feelings."

"Such feelings are no hindrance and all the difference they make is that two will share a microscope."

"But if you tear your clothes, you'll ask one particular girl for a needle, won't you?"

"Yes, that's just what happened to me at first. 'Hey, Katka!' I shouted to her, 'mend my trousers!' And do you know what she said to me?"

"She refused of course."

"More than that: she said, 'Seryozha, I'm surprised at your way of putting it.'"

"What a nice girl! I thought she would have said something rude. I didn't like the way you said 'mend my trousers' at all."

"Yes, she's a sensible girl all right. She brought the question up for discussion by the commune, and the resolution was that since she was so good at sewing it would henceforth be her social obligation to mend our clothes. She agreed to this and mended my trousers willingly enough after that."

"The mending of clothes may become a social obligation, of course, but love is always an individual emotion which is finally sealed by marriage."

The Girl and the Birches

The birches had just put on their flimsy green lace and the woods seemed vast and primeval. To me the train no longer seemed an incongruous monster in these woods, rather the contrary, it seemed highly convenient. I was glad that I could sit by the window admiring the unbroken line of lacy birch woods. By the next window stood a young girl, not particularly good-looking: her forehead was a trifle too high and met the top of her head at almost right angles curving back abruptly in a rather unexpected scholarly manner and suggesting somehow that she worked in a chemist's shop. From time to time she would throw her head back and dart a birdlike look round the car as if a hawk were watching her. Then she would thrust her head out of the window again. I was curious to see what she was like left to herself with the green of the birch-trees. I got up quietly and looked out of the window. She was gazing into the shining lacy green, smiling to herself, whispering something, her cheeks flaming.

The Flowering of the Lungwort

Poplars, aspens, lungwort, mezereon and all the early flowers were in bloom.

My keen interest in and deep sympathy with the changes of nature help me to know beforehand much of what is going to flower, burrow or fly. Sometimes I can even forecast the weather, but in early spring there may be so many changes in the course of a single day that even the fishermen make mistakes.

At dawn the east was clear, while the rest of the sky was a veil of greyish clouds which seemed to be conspiring against the sun. Meanwhile the fishermen were planning their first trip on the lake. The first to come to the waterside was Ivan Ivanovich, the church warden's father. The oldest and most experienced of them all, he acted as something of a barometer for them, though too old to go fishing himself. By the time the others had gathered, Ivan Ivanovich had already come to the conclusion, based on some signs known to him

alone, that the wind would rise later in the day and the fishermen
might be trapped in the floes, and therefore they should not put out
at all.

The fishermen thought hard.

I tried to question them, but their thoughts were more like feelings
and, like nature, had to be studied step by step. All I learnt for certain
was that the ice-roach was on the move, the mud-pike would be the
next, and as to the rest, opinion was divided. To smooth out the
contradictions, the old man remarked gravely:

"You never can tell on the lake."

Against all expectation the sun rose triumphantly, and the fishermen, ignoring the old man's warning, set out along the strip between the ice edge and the southern shore to Uryov where the River
Veksa issues from the lake.

At seven the sun was already peeping out through a gap in the
clouds. A barely perceptible breeze was blowing from the north.

By midday the wind freshened up and it began to hail.

Towards evening a blizzard broke loose in all earnest and our
meadow, just turning green, was white again. The ice pressed against
this side of the lake, and everything happened just as the old barometer had said: the fishermen were trapped by the pack-ice off Uryov.

It was the first evening with no torch-fishing; the whole lakeside
was ice-bound and only a few torches could be seen far to the north
where the water was free.

Dumnov looked at the grey ugly expanse of ice, this unburied
corpse of winter, and observed:

"The bad son-in-law has come to see his wife's mother."

Frost in May

Everything pointed to a sharp frost that night. Soon after midnight
I went out into the oak coppice, where there were always hosts of
tiny birds and early flowers. I had even named this spot the land of
tiny birds and violets.

Soon the first light appeared in the west and kept spreading over
to the east, as if the glow of dawn, unseen below the line of the
horizon, were drawing the afterglow of sunset to itself. Walking briskly
I got so warm that I failed to notice the sharp frost which bound the
grass and early flowers. When the night had ebbed away and the
frost came into its own, I picked one of the tiny violets and tried to

warm it in my palm, but the flower was already brittle and the stalk broke.

The Redwing

The director of the museum was definitely annoyed with the newly-arrived naturalists. He showed me their misspelt entry in the museum book.

"I do not believe illiterates should study biology. What sort of teachers will they make?"

He was right, of course, from his point of view, but I had my own preposterous view on the subject: I was never a very good speller at school. Mathematics did not come easily to me either, its intricacies baffling me. But when twenty-five years later I had to help my son with it, I read straight through his algebra in three days as one might a book of fiction.

Since then this has all been sized up and resolved, and the method by which I completely failed to learn my algebra is known as "ready-made knowledge method" while the method I used later, when the need arose, is called the self-research method, the difference being that in the former method someone instructs one to do this or that, while in the latter the task of the instructor is confined to awakening one's interest.

But this is my own interpretation, while the walls of such a comparatively progressive institution as the Sokolniki Young Naturalists Post display such complicated diagrams of the method, with so many arrows, brackets, and radii that it is as hard to decipher as a problem in spherical trigonometry. I am sure that were this method ever to get to the provinces it would turn into just a corpse of self-research knowledge as dead as the corpse of ready-made knowledge.

"That is what we have to worry about, dear Mikhail Ivanovich," I said to the director, "and not the inability of the lads to spell correctly."

"But they have the impudence to try and teach us!"

"Why take it so seriously? Their task is to size us up as a force."

In the evening the chairman brought a number of test-tubes with different insects and one with some water from Gremyachy Spring. I asked him what he wanted it for. He wanted to test it. When I told him that an analysis had already been made and the result could be found in the museum, he dashed the water out. His efforts had been wasted because according to the self-research method all previous knowledge was to be ignored: a student must find it all out for himself. At school, however, the work is arranged in such a way that the pupil only imagines that he is tackling a problem on his own, while actually it is the teacher who is leading him up to it. That is why in real life it is absolutely essential to learn what has been done in the field by others, or else the same discoveries shall have to be made over and over again.

As we came out, we heard some evening birds singing, undaunted by the wintry landscape.

"Do you know what bird that is?" the chairman asked.

"A thrush."

"But what kind of a thrush?"

"I don't know. What do you think?"

"I won't tell. We have a strict rule at school: if you know, don't tell anybody. Shoot it and find out for yourself."

"But, my dear man," I pleaded, "do make an exception for my sake. I hate shooting a bird out of sheer curiosity, especially when it's singing. I appreciate it first of all as a singer and then as an object for study. Won't you tell me, as one friend to another?"

He thought for a while and said:

"It's a redwing."

No, I couldn't see anything wrong with these lads. I was a great deal worse at their age, though I had a home and parents and was given bromide when my nerves were strained, while these boys had been street urchins and perhaps cocaine-addicts. Palkin had certainly been one.

The Bad Son-in-Law

After a warm night the sun rose hot all at once and amid a complete silence. The lake was again divided in two: the open water in the north and the evil green ragged ice on our side. Soon after dawn a light breeze blew from the south, gradually freshening up, and at midday I heard a shout:

"He's going, he's going away."

"Who's going?" I called from my window.

"The bad son-in-law," Ivan Akimovich replied.

We understood: the ice had been driven away from our side to the overhanging Gremyachy Hill.

The bad son-in-law had gone at last, and the fishermen, marooned for two days and nights somewhere near Uryov, were joyfully returning home in full force, and now we had the live blue splashing on our side of the shore. Fishermen with spears came down to the lakeside. Thousands of gulls flew to the blue and for some reason all settled together, forming a white island not far from the shore; and as usual the blue expanse seemed higher than the level of the town and yet miraculously failed to overflow it. Suddenly the white island broke into hundreds of gulls and the little town peeped through the white wings like the fairy-tale city of Kitezh.

As I watched the shining city, winnowed by the birds, I remembered that the naturalists were to make their report on gulls that day; my children told me that the new-comers had made inquiries about the cost of powder and shot, estimating whether it would be worth while to shoot them all and destroy the pests at last.

All our young enthusiasts would be at the meeting. What if they really took it into their heads to destroy all that beauty?

I went down to the lake and asked an old fisherman whether it was true that the gull was a harmful bird.

"Who told you that?" the fisherman demanded. "Just watch how often they swoop down to the water and come away empty—they don't get much out of it. But just go up into the field and see how many of them are following the ploughman. Why, I heard talk of this sort before. Some people came down from Moscow once and started an argument about which birds were useful and which harmful. They heard a woodpecker drumming nearby and said, 'Just think how much harm it does to the trees.' But we had a learned man of our own here, a doctor, a very fine man indeed, who took them over to that tree and asked, 'Why does this tree wither away?' 'Because the worms bore holes in it,' they said. 'So they do,' he says. 'And the woodpecker gets 'em out. He is not the tree's enemy but its doctor.' So you go up and see for yourself how many gulls are following the ploughman."

The First Mushrooms

The morning was very warm and there was a heavy dew. In the afternoon it drizzled "out of the fleece" but later on it rained quite hard contrary to the common opinion that heavy dew promises fair weather.

The shores of the lake were still under water. In the chocolate-

coloured woods, some of the tree crowns appeared to be decked in
green, while actually it was the green meadows showing through the
bare branches. A white-cheeked wagtail, in its black kerchief and
apron, was frolicking in the puddles near the shore. A sandpiper
kept swinging to and fro. The tufted head of a lapwing poked out
of last year's yellow grass. A drake swam beside his duck.

The road cutting through the woods was becoming impassable, it
could no longer be used that spring. If things went on like this much
longer, the forest would swallow up the road, telegraph poles and
all. Some of the ruts were so deep that streams rushed through them
on rainy days, which naturally deepened the ruts even more. Elsewhere, tall trees had scattered their seed into the ruts, and what had
once been a wheel-track was now an avenue of the most varied saplings with grass and flowers beneath—I had never seen so many
anemones and violets. But how wonderful was the whitish path beaten
by the foot of man! It wound through innumerable bushes of bird-
cherry now bursting into leaf, through hazel and birch saplings. From
time to time a lemon-yellow butterfly hovered into sight. What joy—
to walk along that path! It amazed me why some perfectly healthy
friends of mine chose to go to the Crimea in spring.

The earth was steaming in the sun. The ploughing had begun
for the spring crop. This was just the time for the morel mushrooms.
It was so damp, every step of mine made a smacking sound: it was
like endless kisses. I came out into a clearing and the kisses stopped.
There they were, at last, the mushrooms—right near an old birch
stump with a jolly young fir growing out of the top. As I picked
them I heard a finch bursting into its trills. I was happy—my wish
had come true. I had not gone to the mellow Crimea but had weathered the difficult time to reap my reward: the Crimea had come
to me.

The Meeting

The new-comers opened the meeting by declaring that there was
little chance of qualified research workers coming from Moscow to
direct us in our work. As far as they could see we had enough local
manpower to start with.

Palkin was the first to speak. He told us that we should study only
what could be actually useful; the country was hard-pressed econom-
ically, we could not yet afford the luxury of measuring, say, the size

of the pupils of a toad's eye. The naturalists must concentrate on national economy and materialism.

One of our best local boys could not contain himself at the word materialism.

"Why can't we carry on our studies disinterestedly, without materialism?"

"Dash it!" cried Palkin. "Materialism is not what you can get out of things, but the origin of everything and so on, see?"

"But how can we study all that without instructors?"

"And what about your own brains? Brains are nothing to sneeze at. Use your brains according to our research method and you'll find twenty young naturalists are worth any professor."

This somewhat hazardous interpretation of the maxim about quantity being transformed into quality aroused some murmurs, and a voice could be heard:

"Depends what professor."

Palkin agreed, declaring this was not the point. The point was that we should do away with laxity and remember that our efficiency depended on coordination with the current government plans, and this should be given priority.

After the others had spoken, the chairman gave us an example of how the research method should be applied:

"Take the life of the gull as your topic. Begin your research without reading a single book on the subject. Use the books afterwards merely for reference. First count all the gulls. Here you have the advantage of our collective method. It would be impossible to do this singlehanded, but if you get several schools organized and at a fixed time spread yourselves out over the ponds and the shore of the lake you will be able to do it easily enough."

Thereafter we were supposed to find how much fish the gulls took from the lake and how much they could yield in the way of down and feathers. The feathers were their assets, the consumption of fish the harm they did. We would have to find which was greater. And if the harm outweighed the assets we should have to overcome the local prejudices and destroy the gulls to the last bird. Still, even when destroying them, we had to bear in mind the economic principle, and estimate whether the value of feathers would be worth the expense of shooting.

At this dangerous point I made a friendly suggestion to the chairman that, for fear the sporting temperament of our young naturalists would get the better of their research leanings, it would be not amiss to tell them that "pest" was a relative term. The fox, for example, while doing much harm . . .

The chairman was quite willing and told them that though the fox certainly did some harm to chicken farms, it did much good by keeping down the field mice, and the good by far outweighed the harm. Therefore, on the whole, the fox was a useful animal. Gulls, for their part, devoured insects, and that was a point in their favor.

After this introduction, the general feeling swung in favor of the gulls, and I found it timely to edge in a word or two, suggesting that it would perhaps be better, before undertaking such a complicated piece of research into the value of the gulls and the harm they did, to consult available literature on the subject. Possibly the problem had been solved long ago.

But the most important thing was brought up at the end of the meeting. We discovered that these young naturalists were very good at dissection and so we could learn something from them in this field. Besides they had brought aluminum rings with them to slip on to the legs of the migrating birds. They would be caught somewhere in New Guinea, while we would catch the birds that had been ringed there. Thus people would learn all about the air routes of the birds and this would tell them much about the life of our planet.

THE SPRING OF THE WOODS

Open Water

The life history of a lake is very short. What was once Lake Berendeyevo, the birthplace of the legends about Tsar Berendei, has now become a swamp. Pleshcheyevo, on the other hand, is still very young, and far from getting silted and overgrown, seems to be getting ever younger. Many copious springs rise from the bottom, streams pour into it from the woods, and the Trubezh River carries the remains of the waters of Lake Berendeyevo into it together with the legends about the Berendeyans.

Our learned men have many things to say about the lakes. I am no specialist, of course, and cannot judge their opinions. But is not my own life just like that of a lake in that I also shall die just like the lakes and the seas and the planet and all else? That seems obvious enough and yet, whenever I think of death, the same stupid question arises: "What's to be done?"

I think the reason is that life is stronger than science. It is impossible to live with the same despairing thought, and love of life finds expression only in fairy-tales or in the flippant evasion: "All men are mortal, and I am a man. But never mind—I'll give death the slip somehow." This pitiful facetiousness of ordinary mortals in the face of the inevitable end is brushed aside by the great workaday law of the simple Berendeyans: you may worry about dying but plant your rye just the same.

The insistence of life is immeasurably greater than sheer logic, and so there is no need to fear science. I am no longer young, that's true, but I am as busy as ever and keep my cup brimming full. And as long as I can keep it so, all thoughts of death are empty. Come what may, but of a morning I take pleasure in kindling my samovar, that same samovar which has been serving me from my first meeting with my Lady Berendeyevna twenty-five years ago.

Only on the longest days does the light rise earlier than I, but even then I always get up before the sun, when the ordinary field and forest Berendeyans are still abed. I tip the samovar over the ash-can to shake out yesterday's ashes, then fill it with water from Gremyachy Spring, light the kindlings, and carry it out of doors, leaning its chimney against the wall near the back door. Before it comes to a boil I lay the table for two on the verandah. Then I blow off the specks of charcoal, make the tea and sit down. Now I am no longer an ordinary busy family man but Tsar Berendei himself, admiring his beautiful lake and waiting for the sunrise.

Soon my Lady Berendeyevna comes to tea.

"When was it you cut your beard last?" she says, looking me over critically. "What a sight!"

She chides Berendei, treating him as one of the boys. And Berendei submits without a murmur. They have long passed that stage when the woman is merely a wife. His wife is rather like a mother to him now, and his children like brother-hunters. The time will come perhaps when Lady Berendeyevna will become his granny-wife and his grandsons—his new brother-hunters. A child you were born and a child you shall die—just like the lake: some streams flow in and others out, but as long as one keeps the cup brimming, life is endless.

One by one the Berendeyans appear from the forest, bringing young cockerels, fresh eggs or homespun cloth and lace. Lady Berendeyevna examines all this with great care and occasionally buys something, while Berendei talks with every one of the men: where they live and what they do and what sort of land they have, and whether water and woods are near, and how they dance on holidays and what songs they sing.

A Berendeyan from the Polovetsk District told me that in their swampy forest country they had a road three versts long, and all made of logs: he pressed me to come and take a look at that man-made road. Another Berendeyan from Vedomsha, a pitch distiller by trade, told me in great detail how he split a stump into tiny pieces, distilled the tar, boiled the pitch, and made the turpentine. The third came from Zaladyevo.

"Why do you call it Zaladyevo?" Berendei asked. "What does it mean?"

"We live on the other side of the River Lada,* that's why."

"River Lada, it sounds nice!"

"Doesn't it," the visitor agreed. "We have good grass for mowing there, all along the bank and Utekhin Vrag, and all our villages are well-to-do, even their names have a good, jolly sound."

"Now, we have nothing but stumps, tar, flies and gnats," said the forest Berendeyan from Vedomsha. "Our villages are poor, and the names are grim too."

Rivers and streams, springs and rivulets, water veins and wrinkles, and spots that were merely sweaty—the whole of the land near the lake was a great intricate lacework of water. And Berendei resolved to paddle through them all as soon as Lake Pleshcheyevo was free from ice.

When the sun had passed through all the gamut of the morning colours, and set to its ordinary work in gold, the Berendeyans took themselves off and I was no longer Tsar Berendei.

I drew the curtains in my room and sat down to work. But for some reason or other I could not do anything that day—my thoughts were tangled. My ginger dog Yarik watched me with his fine intelligent eyes, certain that I would not be able to keep this up for long. I succumbed to his look, and soon began a philosophical discussion with him about man and beast: the beast knows everything but cannot put it into words, while the man can put anything into words but does not know everything.

"My dear Yarik, a very wise man once said that the last mystery shall disappear from the earth with the last beast. Horses have already

---

* A maiden from Slavonic folklore.

vanished from the streets of Paris. And they say it is very dull with only motor-cars running about. But look at all the horses we have in Moscow and the birds in the parks. They say there's no other city in the world with as many birds in the streets. Suppose you and I set up a biology post at Botik, and see that all the birds and animals and springs of Berendei are preserved intact for twenty-five versts around. Let Gremyachy Hill be our high school, open only to those few who have proved their ability in creative work, and even then only for a short time—just to prepare them for the great holiday of life in which we shall all join, each adding something new to Berendei's world, and not just littering it with sandwich-wrappings."

I would have gone on talking with Yarik, but my Lady Berendeyevna cried, "Come here, quick, come and look at the lake!"

I ran out and saw something one can see only once in a lifetime, for now the lake was giving me its best and I was giving it mine. The entire heavens with their cities and hamlets, castles and meadows, and modest fleecy clouds stood mirrored in the lake as though on a visit to us, mortals.

I remembered our own springtime when my lady told me: you have taken my best. And I remembered also what she had told me in the autumn when the sun had departed from us, and when, angry at the sun, I had gone out and bought the most powerful oil-lamp to shape life in my own way.

We were all silent for a time, until one of our guests made an inept remark, unable to bear the stillness any longer, "There is a duck over there."

Lady Berendeyevna sighed and said:

"If I had seen this in my youth I would have gone down on my knees."

That was one of those great days in spring when one suddenly realizes why one has borne so many bleak, frosty, and windy days: they were all necessary for the creation of a day such as this.

The First Cuckoo

As soon as I saw that the lake was free of ice, my first thought was that I must go along the shore and into the woods to Usolye, where boats were made.

Everything on our way was just as if the dreams of which I had spoken to Yarik had come true.

On our right, close to the lake, the tall pines rustled and murmured, and on our left lay a wild swampy forest merging with vast marshes. When we entered the pine grove, I noticed some shadows gliding over the sunny patches on the cranberry, and, looking up, I saw that the kites were flying noiselessly from one pine-tree to another.

"It's been so cold all this time," the forester said to us. "But last night it started all at once."

"Still, it was rather chilly at dawn," I remarked.

"But how the birds *clamoured* this morning!" he said.

And at that moment we really heard a clamour which could hardly be recognized as a cuckoo call—it rolled and echoed all across the grove. And even the finches, the tiniest of birds, were making a terrific noise. And the entire grove was clamoring, while the noiseless shadows glided over the cranberry as the large birds flew from tree-top to tree-top.

The First Green Murmur

Towards sunset the western sky was clear but there were a few rumbling clouds in the east, and it was so stuffy that for all we knew a thunderstorm might be gathering. Blue snapdragons were flowering in the fields, and orpine and wild sweet peas in the woods. The fragrant birch leaves glittered stickily in the evening sun. The scent of the bird-cherry in bloom was everywhere. The cranes clamoured and the shepherds blew their horns. The brim and carp came close to the shore.

On our way back we saw a huge glare in the sky: we were afraid it might be our house that was on fire. But it wasn't a fire, and we wondered as people always do on such occasions: what could it be? When the rim of a great disc showed at last, we understood: the moon.

Distant lightning flickered for a long time beyond the lake. There was a light breeze in the woods and we heard the first green murmur.

The First Nightingale

As we were paddling into the lake from the river, from a thicket of willow bushes came a mighty bellow—it was a great bittern with a voice that made you think of an animal the size of a hippopotamus.

The lake was serene again and the water clear because a soothing breeze had been sweeping it all day. The tiniest sound carried far across the water.

We could hear the bittern sucking up the water and then letting out a bellow—once, twice, three times. Then a silence of ten minutes and another bellow, repeated three or four times—but never more than six.

Frightened by the story I had been told in Usolye about a fisherman who had been tossed about by the waves for many hours clinging to the bottom of his capsized canoe, I kept close inshore. I thought I heard a nightingale. Somewhere in the distance the cranes clamoured before going to sleep. We could hear the slightest sound: the whistling ducks whistled here and there, there was a quarrel among the mallards far away, followed by a general hubbub among the ducks, and quite close a wild drake was making love to his mate. Here and there the loons and pochards poked their necks out of the water like false beacons. The white belly of a young pike flashed in the pink waves, and then the black head of the larger one that had seized it.

Then clouds blotted out the sky and I lost my bearings. I steered at random, keeping to the left and trying not to lose sight of the shore looming in the dark. Whenever the bittern bellowed we listened and counted, trying to guess how many times it would be. It was surprising to hear that sound at a distance of two versts, then of three and so on—even after we had rowed more than seven and the singing of innumerable nightingales on Gremyachy Hill was already heard quite distinctly.

May Bugs

The bird-cherry had not yet shed its blossoms and the early willows their seeds, but already the rowan, the apple and the yellow acacia were in flower: they all seemed to be vying with one another. Everything blossomed at once this spring.

The May bugs began to come out in numbers.

In the morning the tranquil waters of the lake were peppered with the pollen of all the flowering trees and herbs. The wake behind my boat was like a path in the forest. And there was a circle wherever a duck had been sitting and a dimple wherever a fish had peeped out of the water.

Forest and lake were in a close embrace.

I walked along the shore to savour the pitchy fragrance of the young leaves. There lay a great pine, its lopped-off branches lying beside it heaped together with aspen and alder twigs, their leaves faded. These disfigured limbs of trees gave off in their decay the most pleasant smell, to the great wonder of bird and beast to whom the secret of living and, moreover, dying fragrantly was a mystery.

The Orioles

The cones on the pines could be seen from afar. The rye had grown to the first knob. The trees, grass and flowers wore their most sumptuous garb. The birds of early spring grew silent: the cocks had hidden themselves away, moulting, and the hens were fasting on their nests hatching their eggs. The animals were busy seeking food for their young. What with sowing and ploughing, the peasants were more harassed than ever.

We saw the coming of the orioles, quails, martins and shore swallows. There was a thick mist after the night's rain, but then it grew sunny though rather chilly. The wind veered before sunset, blowing from our side towards the lake, but the ripples still ran in the same direction for a while. The sun sank into the forest behind a blue cloud, a huge lusterless and ragged ball.

The orioles are very fond of choppy weather. They like the sun to come and go, and the wind to play with the leaves as with waves. Orioles, swallows, gulls and martins have a kinship with the wind.

It was dark since early morning, then it grew stuffy and a large cloud came over. The wind rose and the cloud receded and sank somewhere beyond the lake to the fluting of the orioles and the shrieking of the martins. But the cloud seemed to have gathered strength there, for in the teeth of the wind it came back all black with an enormous white cap. The lake grew troubled: wind fought against wind, wave against wave, and dark patches scudded across the lake like the shadows of wings. Lightning slashed open the opposite shore and thunder pealed. The orioles and the martins fell silent, but the nightingale sang on, and it must have been a large warm raindrop bouncing off his head that made him stop. Rain came down in torrents.

The Martins

After the thunderstorm it suddenly grew very cold and a strong north wind came up. The martins and shore swallows appeared to be spilling themselves from nowhere rather than flying.

That wind blowing day and night, and the hurrying white-crested waves, and the blazing sun, and the tireless scurrying clouds of martins and swallows, and then the gulls flying from Gremyachy Hill, hosts of them, like bluebirds in a good fairy-tale, only not blue but white against the blue. . . . There they were, the white birds, the blue sky, the white crests, the black swallows—and all with the same double purpose, to eat a fellow creature and suffer itself being eaten by another. The midges swarmed and fell into the water, the fish rose after the midges, the gulls darted for the fishes, the minnow for the worm, the perch for the minnow, the pike for the perch, and the fish-hawk from above for the pike.

In the cold dawn, when the wind had abated a little, we set sail before the wind on the molten crests of the fiery waves. Quite close, a fish-hawk swooped down on a pike, but had miscalculated: the pike was the stronger, and after a short struggle, began to submerge. The hawk frantically flapped its great wings but its claws were embedded too deeply, and the voracious fish pulled the no less voracious bird under. The waves impassively carried away a few feathers, effacing all traces of the fight.

In the middle of the lake, where the waves leapt high, we saw a skiff with neither man nor oars or sail.

It was as uncanny as a driverless horse tearing madly for an abyss. Though our canoe was far from safe, we thought of coming nearer and seeing if there had not been some accident, when a man suddenly rose from the bottom of the skiff, took an oar and pulled her to the wind.

We almost shouted for joy. We knew that it was only a tired fisherman who had been taking a nap in the bottom of his boat, but it was like a miracle: we had longed for man to appear, and appear he did.

The Eyes of the Earth

Towards evening it grew so still that the leaves of the birches hardly stirred. An endless stream of people poured down the road below

Gremyachy Hill. When I walked along the sandy track I saw a child's footprints, so tiny and lovable that, had I not been afraid of being laughed at, I really could have stooped to kiss them.

As the peasants walked and drove down the road, their talk was echoed by the calm waters of the lake and reached Gremyachy Hill. Nearly every cart had a young colt running beside it. I heard them saying that potato had all been planted, that some Dmitry Pavlov or other had lost his wife and had not waited the customary six weeks before he married again, he couldn't help it with six little ones to look after. And Marya had married Yakov Grigoryev, she was forty and he sixty, and besides Marya owned a heifer. The people bringing up the rear did not catch what it was Marya owned, and a shout "heifer" went all down the string of carts.

The air was so still now that I could hear a bittern booming in the reeds seven versts away.

And when a peasant woman with her little boy came down to the lake to rinse her washing, and the child, lifting up his tiny shirt, was about to relieve himself in the water, the woman's voice came as clearly as if she were standing beside me:

"Shame on you! You can't do it in your mother's eye."

So she believed that the lake was the eye of Mother Earth. As always I asked Lady Berendeyevna what she thought of it.

"Yes, that is the belief," she said. "And also they switch the meaning on to people. If there's something wrong with a woman's eyes they will say that her little boy must have been relieving himself in the water."

And that is how the old pagan cult disintegrates among the Berendeyans. The poetic image of the eyes of Mother Earth passes into the culture of all mankind, leaving them nothing but a barren superstition.

It was impossible to go to sleep on that scent-weighted night, and the eyes of Mother Earth never closed.

A Mystery of Nature

The finest view of Lake Pleshcheyevo was to be had from Yarilo's Patch on Alexandrov Hill, near which the town of Kleshchin had once stood. At the time the lake had also been called Kleshchino. Prince Yury Dolgoruky rebuilt the town in the marshes near the mouth of the Trubezh River and the new town had inherited the fame of old Kleshchin. The first to be built was the church, which has been preserved to this day and is regarded as a remarkable monument of the twelfth century. So many churches and monasteries have since sprung up around the old cathedral that by studying them one can, with a very few gaps, trace the whole of Russian history from century to century. Now that the lake was ice-free I often boated past the fishermen's settlement to the heart of the town to buy food in the market. The boys did the rowing while I steered, contemplating the ruins of the past. At times this would be quite enjoyable, but I am not very fond of forcing myself into an alien age, and often feel something like rancour for these venerable ruins standing cheek by jowl with monuments to nothing but atrocious taste; to make it worse there would be a bored priest and his wife sitting on a bench near some ramshackle hut, listlessly nibbling sunflower seeds. But I keep a check on these whims of mood and, whenever I go to the market, I ask the fishermen about this or that church and its priest. Once when I was talking to the fishermen about a deserted church, the conversation turned to boats—of the Usolye and Kupan types. To my complaints that it was dangerous going out into the middle of the lake in my light Usolye boat—and I would have liked so much to sail out there—the fishermen replied as one man:

"Go with the *priest* then."

It turned out that the deserted church I had been talking of had stopped functioning just recently. The deacon had been the first to go and the services were conducted by the Priest Filya alone, who seemed quite pleased that the deacon had left. The sexton and the caretaker were the next to go; now Filya sang the responses, swept the church and rang the bells—and was happier than ever. And so he served on cheerfully until all his congregation petered out. And when no one came any more, he took to the lake, ferrying loads of wood and passengers from forest to town.

"Go with the priest, you couldn't do better," said the fishermen. "He'll take you wherever you like—down the Volga or all the way to Astrakhan. He's terribly strong and very good company."

Not a single trip passed after that without some story about the priest: on one occasion he had served with the archbishop for a fee of three rubles; as the Procession of the Cross went through the market-place, Filya saw some unusually large perch sold by one of the fishwomen. This made him forget all about his duties, and he came to his senses only when the procession was out of sight, and he had to race after it in his full vestments. They also said that Filya was always there to help put out a fire, and had saved a lot of lives. Then he fell in love with the lake and became so devoted to it that he refused a large parish, offered him just recently, though his family lived in poverty and his wife had to go to work in the factory.

Little by little I grew so interested in the priest that I began to ask everybody about him. One wise man, a historian, told me that once the priest had defended a group of fishermen at court; the force of his arguments and his insight into the fishermen's psychology were quite extraordinary. He was a remarkable man in every way, the historian said, though altogether unruly.

"Is he a believer?" I asked.

"Just what *is* a believer?" the man said. "He's honest, straightforward, stubborn and trustworthy, but has no intellect. Well, it can't be helped, I suppose. One man is blessed with one thing, and another with something else. The priest is blessed with great strength, and shows no sign of weakening though he's past sixty."

The odd thing was that though I had heard so much about him, it never once occurred to me to ask him to take us for a trip in his boat and tell us the names of the springs and woods and the legends connected with them. It took an intricate chain of events to bring us together and start us on a long trip in his boat.

The Trip with the Priest

Our historian and I had decided to see the pagan ritual known as the Nettle Festival still observed in a rather remote village. I wanted to end my notes on this ritual which takes place when spring's procreative powers reach their climax. We intended to walk to the village across swampy ground and so I ordered a pair of waterproof boots from another very poor priest who made his living as a cobbler. He made it a condition that I go and choose the leather with him. We went to a private shop at the market and as we stood fingering various kinds of leather, a fishwoman came in, bowed to the priest, and asked the shopman whether it was true that the bell had been taken from St. Barbara's and sold.

"Stale news," the shopkeeper said. "They've taken it away to Moscow."

"There are plenty of bells in Moscow," said the woman, "what do they want it for?"

The shopkeeper winked at the priest and said:

"They'll put it up in the Sandunov Baths."

"Stop blethering."

"Who's blethering?" the shopkeeper said.

This seemed to convince her and she asked why they wanted a bell in the baths.

"It's a law in Moscow," he said. "No going to the baths unless the bell tolls."

I paid no attention to the joke of the shopkeeper, who had made it just to please the priest. But when I went to fetch the boots later I heard people talking about it in the market.

"That bell from St. Barbara's refused to go to the baths. The cart broke down, and it got stuck in the middle of the road. 'Why did you sell me to the baths?' it said. 'I won't go.' And it didn't. They looked it over then and found that it had hung on its smaller lug because the larger one was broken, and if they hadn't moved it from the belfry it would have been all right, but they couldn't hang it on its smaller lug at the baths. And so the people from Moscow said, 'We don't want it like that, take it back.' But our people at the museum told them, 'Why didn't you look before you bought it? We've got the money for it and it's none of our business now.' "

I then went to the museum and learned that, having no historical value, the bell had indeed been sold to a village in the Moscow Province, and that it was quite true that it had crashed on the way and that the larger lug had been found to be broken. But no issue had been raised and the bell had been taken on to its destination.

We laughed and I suggested that it wouldn't be bad at all if the museum gave us, say, ten rubles of the "bell" money to finance our excursion. It turned out that we could get twice as much, and could therefore go a little farther along the bank of the Kubra: there was Long-Awaited Hill somewhere in that neighborhood, where, according to the chronicles, the Suzdal and Novgorod armies had fought the famous battle which unexpectedly proved the supremacy of the Suzdal people and marked the birth of Greater Russia. Traces of the battle might be found in Long-Awaited Hill; it would be worth excavating. We would do well to take along some of our young naturalists and Sergei Sergeyevich, our zoologist, to study the fauna of the Kubra. Besides, we had among us a young artist, a photographer, a botanist and a geologist.

One thing followed another until we ended up with a regular expedition. We were too many for one cart, and even two, and we now estimated our expenses to be no less than fifty rubles, but even that seemed not enough. At last Mikhail Ivanovich had a brain-wave.

"Let us all go in a large boat," he said.

Incidentally, his motive had nothing to do with cutting down our expenses at all, but with the fact that this was the ancient waterway of peoples in the time long past, who had left us their neolithic settlements, ruins of cities, and burial mounds on the shores.

"We'll go with the priest," voices called out at once.

We began our preparations, and whatever the others might have thought, the idea of our expedition was inseparably linked in my mind with the unusual priest's personality.

Perch on the Move

If we had called our trip into the depths of Pereslavl Uyezd an excursion, we could hardly have attracted our youngsters because the word smacked too much of school. And so we called our journey an expedition, and not only our junior naturalists joined us but also a few of the students whom we called the Robinsons, to distinguish them from the younger pathfinders. Under the guidance of their elders, our pathfinders drew up maps, learned to measure altitudes with a barometer and calculate the flow of a current, stuff and ring birds, and so on. The Robinsons were out for adventures mostly, and their preparations had a practical aspect. Petya succumbed to their influence and took to making fishing-rods: he planned to keep the expedition supplied with fish and decided to have a try at deep water angling which was a new sport to him. It had been raining since early morning and when it cleared I saw four boats anchored off Nadgorod. Petya now joined them, and the boats seemed very small—just five flies. The sun soon disappeared, and the water on the other side of the lake was like silver and on our side like steel. The wind rose again and everything darkened. A huge cloud came up and the silver turned to cast iron seething with a white froth. The boats were bobbing in and out of sight on the iron water, and then a heavy rain hid them completely.

I waited patiently under a tree on Gremyachy Hill for the light to come back; when the sky cleared after the rain and the boats came into sight one by one, I went home relieved. That day the rain came and went four or five times, the boats disappearing each time. Petya came home dripping wet, and we had soup with the perch he caught.

The Robinsons

We met every three days and discussed our plans. Each of our specialists had his own subject. I alone had none. I simply use my innate ability to combine experiences and impressions gained from life and books and fuse them into what is commonly known in fiction as the hero. The hero, after all, is always fashioned out of the author, his own thoughts and feelings. I differ only in that I impart these thoughts and feelings not to a fictitious person but to a given locality and so it becomes a living being, as it were. I was sure this simple method would not fail me this time either. The combined efforts of scientists studying the locality, each in their own narrow field, could never draw up a picture as descriptive as mine. And therefore I regarded myself on a par with the scientists of our expedition.

While we were discussing our subjects, our young naturalists, both Robinsons and pathfinders, kept very quiet. But as soon as we turned to the practical side of the expedition the Robinsons immediately came to the fore. First of all, they announced that Father Filya's large lake boat would not come through the shallows with all fifteen of us and our equipment aboard. Instead, we should have to take at least four river boats. But without our brawny priest, we should have to do all the rowing ourselves and that would mean so much less time for science. After a lengthy debate we decided to take the priest's boat but put no more than seven men in it, accommodating the rest in two lighter boats. Then there was the matter of oars. We lacked the training to row with the fishermen's heavy oars for any length of time, and so we needed lighter ones. Mikhail Ivanovich suggested drawing upon the bell money again, but the students balked at the expense and, well versed in lake-lore from childhood, decided to go to the forest, fell a tree and make the oars themselves. There was little talk about tents and instruments—we had easily enough found a barometer, an anemometer cup, some thermometers, a drag, nets and guns.

But there was another problem: could we do any fishing with a drag-net in the closed season? Said the students, "Who's going to lay

down the law for us in the wild marshes?" Another problem: could
we shoot a moulting drake or grouse in the closed season if the need
arose? The Robinsons answered that we could kill a village ram in
an emergency, let alone a miserable wild duck. Finally, they decided
not to waste any money on buying a cauldron for cooking but take
two ordinary buckets.

We, the older men, exchanged looks, and someone remarked, "We're
certainly in for a jolly trip."

The Departure

I was to start right from Botik with all the pathfinders and one
Robinson to meet the rest at Uryov. Petya went to the fishermen's
settlement to fetch my boots and brought back some alarming news:
two delegates from the Robinsons had come to Father Filimon to fix
row-locks on his boat for the lighter kind of oars, but he would not
have his boat spoiled, and when they insisted he lost his temper and
flatly refused to go at all.

My pathfinders went to bed greatly troubled. If the priest wasn't
coming it would hardly be fun going at all. Thus before we had even
seen him, the priest came to join our expedition as a fabulous sort
of figure.

A thin dusting of pollen from the trees and meadows lay over the
water in the early morning, and the lake looked as if it could do with
a good brushing. Our boat left an indelible wake through it, the birds
left a trail too, and whenever a fish rose it made a dimple on the
surface.

The sun was spilling all its rays on the lake and Yarilo's Patch stood
clearly mirrored in the water: a very good omen because, as I saw it,
the main purpose of the expedition was to discover the surviving
remnants of the cult of the Slavonic god of fertility.

The lake lay perfectly still under the white veil of morning, and
the boat we saw in the distance looked like a fly crawling across a
white sheet. Could it be Father Filimon? No, the boat was too small.
And there should have been two boats anyway.

We had already passed Botik, Kuroten, and the whole of Zakhap
when we caught sight of the priest's boat on the far side of the lake
opposite Alexandrov Hill. It stood out clearly against the still waters,
with the Robinsons' small boat flying a red pennant a little ahead.
Both were keeping close inshore, the priest wielding his one heavy

oar and the Robinsons rowing with broad swings. So Filya had his own way after all, and did not let them put row-locks on his boat. They were coming on at good speed and, as we had lost some time chasing a loon in the reeds, we discovered we had about the same distance to cover to Uryov. Our lads plied their oars and very soon I saw the famous priest working at the rudder of his long dug-out. He was a tall gaunt man in a grey coat and straw hat. His beard was a nondescript colour, turning grey most probably. In short, a priest like any other but for the red flag. The bow of his boat was heaped high with various traps and our botanist Sergei Sergeyevich was already ensconced there, busily catching insects with his butterfly net. Mikhail Ivanovich sat amidship, as important as a queen bee. In front of him sat Boris Ivanovich, the young artist, paddling hard to help Filya, while a serene old man with a white beard had one of the side seats.

We all reached Uryov together, and learned some bad news when we landed: the geologist had not arrived from Moscow and so we were left without the camera plates he had promised to bring along. The botanist had also backed out. But our disappointment dimmed before the glad news that Academician Spitsin, the famous archaeologist, had come quite unexpectedly, and we would do our excavating of sepulchral mounds and settlements of prehistoric man under his supervision. So this was who the serene old man was.

I was especially happy because until then there had been two serious gaps in my experience: I had never flown in a plane and had never done any excavating with an archaeologist. And now here we were going to delve into the mysteries of the earth guided by Spitsin himself, and so one of my dreams would soon come true.

The New Canal

What were we to call our dug-outs bestowed the honour to make this remarkable voyage along the Nerle and Kubra? Naturally enough our junior naturalists' vessel came to be called the *Pathfinder*, while the students' boat was as obviously christened *Robinson*, but there was heated discussion as to the name of the third. Some wanted to christen it *Popadya*, others *Matushka*, while a third party insisted on *Badya*.*

---

* The first two are the popular names for a priest's wife; the latter means a "tub" and rhymes in the joke that follows.

"Why *Badya*?" asked the priest.

"Haven't you heard the one about the priest who made a *badya* out of his *popadya*?" said one of the Robinsons.

The priest listened leaning on his oar, tall and spare, smiling with wrinkles as deep as saber cuts. He was obviously enjoying himself.

Mikhail Ivanovich, however, decided that *Tub* would cast a slur on Father Filimon's old lady's present occupation and suggested the name of the *Frigate Pallada*. Finally we decided that the boat should be tentatively christened *Matushka*, but that we should all do our utmost to earn the *Matushka* the imposing name suggested by Mikhail Ivanovich.

Meanwhile the zoologist was already hunting with his butterfly net among the growth on the bank. He beamed when he inspected the contents: the yield was unusually good, and he had caught many of the specimens he was looking for. He emptied the net into his photo-collector: the beetles crawled towards the light, falling into the jar. Some of the Robinsons went to do some fowling, while others under the zoologist's supervision collected water beetles and seeds floating in the water. The pathfinders took the barometer reading, floated their current gauges and began to calculate the width of the estuary.

So this was a real expedition and not just a school excursion, for everything was done in all earnest and not as mere scholastic make-believe. Every fact we registered—the current's speed and the width of the river—was new and useful. We also discovered that Uryov was not an individual name, but the name given by the local people to the estuaries of all rivers emptying into lakes. Veksa was not a proper name either but was given to any river connecting two neighboring lakes, in this case Pleshcheyevo and Syomino.

Leaving the lake, the Veksa makes a sharp bend and then another and a third, and turns upon itself so closely that people boating down parallel bends can almost shake hands across the narrow strip between. And yet nobody ever thought of digging a canal through one of these strips. We decided to begin our journey with a try at canal-digging on a small scale. The priest was especially keen for he often had to struggle through the maze of sharp curves when delivering wood. He said he would have dug a canal long ago had he not been afraid of the local people: they were too suspicious and superstitious and quite capable of repaying his good work with a drubbing. We were through in about twenty minutes, working with our shovels and oars, and the water rushed in to link the two curves. The pathfinders' boat came through easily as did the Robinsons', but *Matushka* ran aground halfway and blocked the current. We all set to and hauled her free, and when the boat was through, the water gushed in, cutting off the tip of the curve into a tiny island.

"If anybody had done this before I would not have grudged him a five-kopek piece of my own money," said the priest, greatly delighted.

So we called the island Five-Kopek Piece, and the new canal the Pathfinders' Canal.

Sergei Sergeyevich added to the occasion by reading his "March of the Pathfinders" which he had composed the day before, and the Robinsons, fitting the words to the tune of the Marseillaise, rowed ahead chanting behind their red pennant:

> Row on to glory, nature-lovers, row on
> To glory, forward, march!

In short, it was very jolly.

"Isn't the weather fine," the archaeologist observed.

"And I have a pain in my leg, that's a sure sign of changing weather!" the priest replied.

A Settlement of Primitive Man

The island formed by the greater Nerle and Kubra rivers, that desolate expanse of marshy forests, is almost as uninhabited now as it was thousands of years ago in the days of neolithic man, who made his way down streams away from this fearful spot, settling only where there were fish or game to be caught. It was just along these marshy tributaries of the lakes that we had to go to reach the first dry patch where today's fishermen landed and built their fires; and it could be said almost for certain that the neolithic fishermen had their settlement there, too, and must have left traces of primitive culture.

Going down the Veksa, we landed on the first spot dry enough to walk on, and in the limpid water we saw a darker layer of soil, quite possibly of a much later origin. This clearing was now called Little Field because it had been under the plough some time ago. Even before we landed, our pathfinders and Robinsons, who had heard so much about the recently discovered and as yet unexplored settlement of primitive man, fished out of the water a scrap of pottery, a fragment of flint bearing the traces of man's handiwork, and a macrolithic tool. In Little Field itself we found the moles had done our exploratory work for us. We scattered over the meadow examining the dark mole-hills, every one of which yielded either a piece of pottery, a flint scraper, an arrowhead, an axe or a stone chisel. These treasures dug up by the moles decided the archaeologist at once.

"The thing is clear enough, we must begin excavating. I've never seen anything like it in Russia."

For that matter, not many settlements have been excavated in Russia anyway. No more than a hundred in the whole vast country.

The digging is usually started by one man using an ordinary spade. Lyova was digging with such ecstasy that he might soon have come out at the other end of the earth. But it was not long before the subsoil and water appeared.

"Now cut the soil with this tool just as if you were slicing cheese," the archaeologist told him.

The way he did it now we could clearly see the sections: a dark top layer, then sand, then another dark layer and sand again. That intermediate dark layer is called the burial soil.

"This burial soil belongs to the earlier Stone Age, doesn't it?" Lyova asked brightly.

"So we presume," replied the archaeologist.

He walked to the bank of the river where he discovered the mouth of another stream overgrown with rushes, then into the woods inspecting everything thoroughly.

"This spot may have been the shore of Lake Pleshcheyevo," he said as he came back.

The Robinsons and pathfinders listened with awe.

"How many thousands of years ago could that have been?" Lyova asked eagerly.

"I'd rather not talk in thousands," said the old pathfinder. "Suppose we say it was a long time ago."

"What was our country like in those days?"

"Previously there were only lakes and no rivers, then for some reason there was a great increase of moisture until the shores could not withstand the pressure and the water broke through. And so the rivers began to flow. That is how the Volga started: it has been proved. Probably this lake too began to overflow in the same manner. The early men gathered on the lake shores and rivers to fish. That was the earlier Stone Age. When the lake shore became the river-bank, the site was no less suitable for fishermen. If the pottery we find in the top layer of later origin looks newer we shall say that it belongs to the later Stone Age. So there's no point, children, in talking about thousands of years but only about which is a bit older and which newer. The finds themselves are of less interest to me now than the layer they happen to be in. Well, Lyova, start your slicing and keep your finds in four groups. Those from the first layer on this side, from the second over there, and so on. And don't forget to spread some paper for them before you begin."

The spade struck against something almost immediately and Lyova handed the professor a small piece of pottery, with pocks as large as peas, holding it gingerly and reverently as if it had been a precious gold vessel of a Scythian tomb. I was not sure, either, if I did not prefer this crude fragment to the Scythian gold of the Hellenistic era.

The old scholar examined the piece closely, almost caressing it.

"This is a pretty old one," he said happily.

"And what about this one?"

"Much newer. See this net pattern? It shows it is much newer, but not bad either. We have few of the newer samples as yet."

Our youngsters soon noticed that though the newer samples were perhaps more valuable for science, the older things were more to the taste of the old scholar, and tried their best to find as many of them as they could. They picked up the jargon in a matter of minutes, and were talking briskly about ceramics, and sorting out the fragments according to cultures: Fatyanov culture, the Dyakov type.

"If the name of the culture comes from the site where the finds are made, we might yet have Pereslavl culture, mightn't we?"

"Quite possibly, but the site will become famous anyway."

We used the same tree-forks the fishermen had used to hang our tea-kettle over the fire. As we drank our tea we noticed now a fishbone left by a present-day fisherman, now a piece of pottery dented by a neolithic man. Meanwhile the old scholar was busy sorting out the fragments by cultures, handling the various flints and macrolithes so skilfully that he might have himself lived in the Stone Age and used those same flint tools.

"Isn't this the mark of an early man's finger-nail?" asked one of the pathfinders.

"It may be. Everything was done by hand in those days and the women must have done most of the work."

"Why women?"

"We can tell that from the ornaments. Where there are ornaments, there are sure to be women. Besides, we can sometimes tell by the fingerprints."

"In that case, this mark certainly is the trace of a finger-nail."

"Why certainly? Just say—quite possibly."

"But who were they, those people?"

"We don't know. We still don't know what they were like, or even their name."

The scholar began to speak guardedly of his surmises, and it was clear that this was the dream of his life—to learn something of that mysterious race.

While we sat listening, Father Filya went wandering about—he had an urge to act for himself and to discover something on his own. His face beaming, he returned with an unusual find.

"Here you are," he said, holding out a small round object. "It's the spout of a teapot. So they drank tea too."

The archaeologist explained that far from drinking tea, they barely knew enough to kindle a fire from a tree set ablaze by lightning in those days. Those clay vessels were not used for cooking but merely for keeping food and water.

Father Filimon listened with respect but it was clear that a stubborn question worked in the depths of his unruly mind: "But who has seen all this?"

A layman governed by instinct, he actually had to see a man's features to be able to talk about him. He refused to think in terms of ceramic fragments, piecing it all together, as scholars did. He pictured primitive man in his own likeness.

We laughed about the teapot, but I wondered if Father Filimon wasn't partly in the right, at least in principle. Did not the scholar demonstrate the uses of different tools by imitating present-day handicraftsmen—masons, carpenters and blacksmiths? But to be bolder still, supposing we could trap the creative spark on a modern man's face and transfer it to that of the genius who had once had the brilliant idea of using fire, so that his hairy face, with the stamp of genius, should contrast even more sharply with that of a present-day ape with the creative spark gone.

It's fascinating, this excavating! I should have liked to reflect on and on but I noticed the mist rising over the river and suggested moving on. Perhaps we could find another settlement on Lake Syomino which would, who knows, reveal something of the Bronze Age.

Primitive Man

Just opposite Little Field on the other bank of the Veksa there was a magnificent grove of tall pines, some of them leaning over the water, with their roots almost upturned, threatening to fall and capsize a boat sailing past. The river continued its winding course between the banks overgrown with pines, doubling back, its bends almost parallel. In times of yore a Novgorod merchant would keep tacking along the bends, safely pass the pine-grown steeps, find himself between banks so swampy there was no chance of landing, and finally reach an island with a tall bush close to the water, and lurking behind it—a thief. This fear of the bush survived in the name of the locality—Thieves' Bush. But we passed the overhanging pines safely and no one attacked us from behind the bush. And now Usolye came in sight, the famous village known in the history of Greater Russia for its salt. There was Goats' Hill near the bank, where we saw the unmistakable traces of the famous salt quarries which used to supply salt to the whole of Russia.

At Usolye we came upon the first mill dam where we had to unload our boats and drag them overland. While we were busy with this tiresome task, the local peasants gathered around, marvelling at our guns, our bags, the priest and the red flag, wanting to know who we were and what we were up to. When we told them one of the men asked:

"And what is the sense of it all?"

Meanwhile Sergei Sergeyevich was asking another group of peasants about the field and wood pests and epizootic diseases, and his lively talk appealed to everybody. So when a new man joined in and once more asked what was the sense of it all, his fellows told him derisively, "No sense for you unless it jingles."

After twisting and turning along the river bends for more than an hour, yet never losing sight of Usolye, we at last pulled into the dwindling lake of Syomino, about one and a half versts long. The water was no deeper than an oar-blade but the slime below lay so thick that you could not touch hard bottom with an oar. In an emergency it would be impossible to swim here for the slime would suck one in. In short, a dangerous spot, a duck's paradise.

As on the Veksa, the first dry spot where we could land, and where the fishermen generally landed, turned out to be a neolithic settlement. The right corner of this lake-swamp where the dry spot stood out as conspicuously as a cake on a table, had once been a Market-Place. Some Sadko* or other, a rich merchant from Great Novgorod, must have sailed here—from his grain-hungry North to this granary of the Suzdal land. He must have cooked his fish soup here just as we did, oblivious, however, to the Stone Age relics dug up by the moles. They were not interested in ancient pottery in those days.

Our Robinsons put up two tents, while the priest made a fire, hanging up a bucket for the gruel, and we settled on a log in the smoke to keep the mosquitoes away. By the fading light the zoologist was busy mounting his beetles on cotton.

"A bat!" he suddenly shouted. "We haven't got one in the museum, shoot it!"

And we began the tricky sport of shooting bats in the dusk.

A resin torch flashed on the lake, then a boat pulled in and two fishermen came up carrying spears. All fishing, and torch-fishing too, was forbidden in this month, but nobody minded the law, of course, in such a desolate place. Our red flag made them wary, though, and so they wanted to find out who we were. They told us that the most important fish in this overgrown lake was not the tough kind, such as pike or perch, but the soft kind—tench and carp. In addition to the usual methods of fishing they had their own ways for muddy overgrown lakes. One of these was known as "by boil." One kept pushing an oar into the mud until the fish was scared out of the slime, leaving a track of bubbles, just as if the water were boiling. The fish was traced by these bubbles and down went a net or a spear. Another trick, called "by mud," was much the same, except that the clue lay in the disturbed mud instead of the bubbles. And a third method was called "by grope," that is, simply fishing by groping.

One of the fishermen, Pavel by name, told us all this in a very brief and graphic manner. Others would have used a long sentence where he merely said:

"One poke and a pikelet bubbled."

I told our youngsters that his vivid speech was the best for describing nature observations.

The two fishermen had a sort of family resemblance to each other, though Pavel's eyes were large, grey and wistful while Nikolai's were mere slits. Pavel rarely smiled, while Nikolai was always chuckling.

---

* A legendary merchant from Russian folklore.

Pavel made several attempts to catch one of the bats by hand, while Nikolai ducked and shuddered every time one came his way.

We discovered that Pavel had read the book on Pereslavl written by Mikhail Ivanovich and some other books as well. Not far away, he told us, at a place called Barmazovo on Stulov Hill, there was a large group of hummocks that looked like burial mounds, also there was an ancient graveyard near the village of Khmelniki with two mounds in it. Nikolai had tried digging in one of them and it really proved to be a burial mound. He had been looking for buried gold and, seeing a round object, he pounced upon it and then froze with horror: the thing was a skull. He dropped it and took to his heels. Pavel buried the skeleton and somebody put a wooden cross over it later on. It had happened a year ago but Nikolai was still afraid to go near the place.

Ignoring Nikolai's presence, Pavel concluded quietly and distinctly:

"We forest people are as stupid and superstitious as primitive man."

His words reminded me of my thoughts about primitive man at Little Field.

"What makes you think primitive man must have been stupid and superstitious?" I said. "People were probably as different then as we are now. Take yourself, for instance. Though you come from almost a primitive forest village, you have a sober mind and Nikolai's superstition seems stupid to you."

"I turned out to be a man apart somehow," said Pavel. "I read a lot when I was at school."

This news about the burial mounds could not be ignored and we decided to set off the next morning in a body for Barmazvo and make a thorough investigation. Pavel volunteered to help with the digging and Nikolai joined him. We warned Nikolai that we were interested not in gold but in skeletons, yet he insisted that he would help us anyway.

It was pitch dark when we settled for the night in our two tents: the older men and some of the pathfinders in the smaller and the Robinsons and the priest in the larger one. Sergei Sergeyevich was the only one who had a felt sleeping-bag into which he crawled, while the rest lay down on tarpaulins, covering themselves with coats and whatever else there was. We had to admit we were not properly equipped. Sleeping that way was pretty awful, but the possibility of wind or rain was more awful still.

"The barometer fell six points today," Sergei Sergeyevich remarked from out of his bag.

"My leg is getting worse," the priest added.

I don't think I slept more than two hours that night and even then my half-thoughts and half-sensations kept hovering around Stone Age man. He appeared to me not as the apelike creature we were told of at school but as an embodiment of the difference between the two fishermen Pavel and Nikolai. To my mind, in the process of creation Nikolai had been discarded as having served his purpose and destined to exist unchanged, while Pavel went on developing. In his own background Pavel too was discovering fire just as his ancestor of genius. In short, one was a man and the other an ape, but since the skulls and fragments were sure to be absolutely the same, it would be impossible afterwards to say which of the two had given an impetus to life's movement and which had merely existed. The only purpose, as far as I could see, for collecting skulls and pottery was to get a better insight into the mentality of early man. But to achieve this, we ought to study the mentality and strivings of modern man just as closely. And of all the members of our expedition our professor had possibly come nearest to understanding the mentality of early man.

The skull walls in our brain, as it were, and we, used to working indoors, create a double skull for ourselves. When spending a night in the open we suddenly find that the mind works in infinite spaces—yet too haphazardly, spreading like the wind and the rain. And when a cold rain begins to patter, our thoughts undergo a swift change.

I looked through a chink in the door-flap. The sky was overcast, there was a cold drizzle and only the fresh green of the trees showed that it was spring and not autumn. I was about to close my eyes again and sink into my half-thoughts about early man when the flap of the other tent went up and I saw a shaggy head with a matted beard of a nondescript colour and the keen eyes of a forest dweller set in a creased weather-beaten face. It would surprise me if this priest who had come back to nature would begin his day with a prayer: why leave church then? And he didn't. Paying no attention to the drizzle, he crawled out of the tent in his jacket and boots, pulled on his priest's robe, at once becoming a real priest, and stooped to an ember of yesterday's fire, trying to blow it to life. He was skilful and ingenuous, shielding the fire from the rain first with his hand and then with a frying-pan, which he afterwards rigged up over the blaze. Then he peeled some potatoes, put them in the pan to fry and began to clean the roach which he must have gotten from the fishermen the day before. After eating one panful, he made himself another, then rolled a huge cigarette of home-grown tobacco and lay on his stomach, oblivious to the damp beneath him and drizzle above. He lay there enjoying his smoke and watching the lake, content, happy and free, blending unthinkingly with the universe.

Poking my head out of the tent, I called to him softly, not to disturb his beautiful repose:

"Father."

"What is it?" He did not even turn his head.

"I've been watching you and wondering why you went to all that trouble of rigging up the pan when you could have made some soup in the pot."

"Roach is a lonely fish in soup," he answered readily.

"You mean bony?"

"No, lonely. Roach is only good for frying. Roach soup makes you brood, you keep worrying about your family at home and what the future will bring. It's a lonely fish."

"But perhaps it's not the fish that makes you brood."

"What else then?"

"Well, many things—dissatisfaction, troubles. . . ."

"No, I'm past troubles now. I carry the firewood, row for the fishermen, and cut the timber—I've no troubles, no complaints. But ask the fishermen, they'll say the same. You can't make a fish soup from roach. It's a lonely fish."

The older men knew it was raining by the noise and dampness, and were too disappointed to get up, but when they heard us talking about the lonely fish they all laughed and felt happier. Our talk with Father Filimon came to an end.

The Origin of Man

Stulov Hill, where Pavel and Nikolai brought us, nestled in the Barmazovo woods not far from the road of logs, actually a bridge over the swamp three versts long, and the beginning of the road to the Polovetsk District. To the right of the log road meandered the stream known as the Chertoroi coming up and burrowing into the swamp again, and still further to the right the River Lada flowed through the bluish woods; and the land beyond, the most primeval stretch in those parts, was called Zaladyevo. Barmazavo had once been one of the most flourishing and densely populated spots here. But in the times of Ivan the Terrible famine and misfortune carried off many and scattered the rest, leaving the forest to reign supreme. The older people said that a wooden church had been completely grown over by the woods and that the bells had sunk into the swamp. The righteous could sometimes hear the chimes of the sunken bell.

The stony mounds on Stulov Hill were oblong in shape and by all appearances were burial mounds, but when the archaeologist checked their direction by compass, it turned out that they lay from south to north instead of from east to west. Still human agency was so obvious here that we decided to start digging.

As we wanted to learn the correct way of digging, each was assigned his task from the outset. Mikhail Ivanovich was put in charge. He measured the mound with his tape, drew the plan, established the line which divided the ground proper from the mound soil—known as the belt among the archaeologists—calculated the position of the grave's edge and generally looked after the scientific aspect of the work. The academician, acting in the modest capacity of foreman, took his post on the mound, showing the others where to cut a trench across it.

We removed one rock after another, each time hoping that the earthen mound would soon be revealed. Though the sand did appear, it quickly changed to rocks and again we had to pry them off. It drizzled all the time, we were wet through and covered with mud from head to foot.

"I've never come across such a difficult mound yet," remarked our learned foreman.

"It is a mound, is it?" asked Lyova.

"It is certainly the work of man."

And again we pried off stone after stone. Nikolai suddenly remembered that there was a hole in the roof of his hay-loft which had to be mended at once or the rain would spoil all his hay. He hurried home, but Pavel carried on. Lyova had great faith in the professor, and was sure that the skeleton would be found.

"What if this is only a glacial deposit?"

"It's unlikely, but deserves consideration."

The scientist walked to similar mounds nearby, took measurements and stood there calculating thoughtfully. We got rid of the last stone and completed the trench across the mound. Though we had dug well into the subsoil there was no belt at all—nothing, except a fir cone about the size of a little finger which we seized upon eagerly and examined at great length. Mikhail Ivanovich stood there, wet and miserable. I was sorry for him and asked about his daughter.

"Sonya's gone to take her entrance exams to the Moscow Art School," he said, brightening.

Lyova kept saying angrily that we were sure to find the skeleton since Alexander Andreyevich had said that this was a burial mound.

"No, Lyova," the archaeologist replied, emerging from the woods. "This is not a burial mound."

"Then we've been digging for nothing?"

"Not at all. We have proved that it is not a burial mound."

"What is it then?"

"It's hard to say, it requires a special investigation. That can be done afterwards. But there's no doubt it was the work of man, though."

That is how science moves on. Even the negative results are necessary and valuable. But we felt as if we had gone to the North Pole, expecting to find something extraordinary and finding nothing at all but sheer abstractions such as sextant or barometer readings.

The mystery of the Barmazovo woods was to remain unsolved. We ate some bread and strawberries and went down to Khmelniki where there were several burial mounds and an ancient graveyard near the Chertoroi River. On the way there Pavel showed us a few huts in the dense forest near the Zheltukhino swamps where deserters had once lived: we could tell from the shavings lying about that they had occupied themselves with woodwork of some kind. After the deserters, the huts were used by illegal vodka distillers: we could still see the holes they had dug for their stills.

The sight of the ancient graveyard cheered us a little. It was a typical Novgorod cemetery, and its location—far from Novgorod but close to the Market-Place, on the road to the rich cornfields of Opolye—was significant to a local historian. Nearby there was the flattened mound which Nikolai had searched for treasure and another, untouched, next to it. The waters of Lake Syomino glimmered through the tree-tops.

This time, everything was as it should be: it was a typical burial mound with a hollow nearby from which the earth had been taken to pile up the mound. The direction, checked by compass, was from east to west and the trench-digging was begun from the south, which makes it easier to find the belt. No sooner had we removed the top soil than huge rocks confronted us, and we had to pry them away one after another in the never ending rain.

The pathfinders worked over the graveyard, and Lyova and Pavel over the mound. It was getting dark but there was still no belt—only another great rock to pry away. Pavel went home on some urgent business, and Lyova carried on alone. I knew him well. He had been working beyond his strength, but once he had keyed himself up, he would never stop: the skeleton must be found. Suddenly a large stone came rolling down and bruised his right hand, incapacitating our last manual worker. Once again the scholar walked away and stood there thinking hard. We were so muddy, hungry and tired that we no longer believed this was a burial mound at all. Very pale, Mikhail Ivanovich sat on a stump by a pine.

"What are you thinking about, Mikhail Ivanovich?"

"I'm worried about Sonya's exams."

He and I discussed on the quiet how best to tear the tireless professor away from his mound so that we could go to Pavel's cottage, have something to eat, drink some tea and go to sleep in his hayloft. Had he a hayloft?

The archaeologist came up just then.

"A pimple," he said.

This meant that if the mound looked like a pimple on the surface of the earth from the distance, it was sure to be a tomb.

It was getting quite dark and we asked the professor if we could stop work for the day.

"All right," he said. "We shan't be long now. Give me the spade, Lyova. Let me have a go at it."

He disappeared in the trench. His grey head bobbed up and down as he dug. Then his spade struck a peculiar sound and his grey mop vanished altogether.

"Will you come here, Lyova. Take the spade and tap this spot. Did you hear that? It could only be a bone."

"A bone!"

We sprang to our feet. We felt like hunters to whom success gives a new surge of strength. But this was more than hunting. It was the triumph of the ultimate effort of men of science in search of truth, which puts them above mere hunters and distinguishes the explorer among all others, and which had once set apart from the world of apes the primeval scientist who learned to obtain fire. In the features of our scholar at that moment I could see the face of our forebear, the primeval man of genius, the one with a hairy body, iron will, a light in his eyes and a heart with love and tenderness hidden in its depths.

It was a thigh-bone, long and dark. We covered it with earth and left it lying across the trench. We jauntily went to Pavel's cottage. So in science it does not take a grand display to make men happy: sometimes a little bone will do.

News of our find soon spread around the village and as we sat drinking our tea at Pavel's, the peasants kept coming in. They sat and listened, while we did the talking.

We talked over our tea as the educated usually do, never realizing what a wealth of knowledge and experience gained through generations cropped up in that simple discussion. But the people listening to us were children of the soil.

We talked about north and south, and bandied the millenniums like so many days; we skimmed over the earth itself, while some trifle discovered in a mound would keep us absorbed for a long time. Our archaeologist told us that once, while excavating with an expedition somewhere in the south, a student with a keen eye for that sort of thing detected a tiny, badly worn coin, their only find apart from the bones; and that this little coin, a trifle to all appearances, had made the rounds of many scholars who tried to identify it with a holy fear of wearing it away completely, thus depriving science of the only reliable testimony of a whole epoch. It was finally dipped in caustic soda and found to belong to the tenth century.

"Tenth, did you say?" one of the peasants asked. "I've got a much older coin: seven hundred and twenty-one."

"What does it look like?" asked the archaeologist in surprise.

"A big copper one, like a five-kopek piece."

The professor laughed: "If anybody found a coin like that he would get a million for it."

We all rose and went to the hayloft for the night. The others soon settled down but I sat on a log in front of the house, smoking and talking to Pavel. I was curious to know how much of our discussion the peasants had grasped.

"You see that scrap of cloud melting away up there?" said Pavel. "That's the way thoughts melt in their minds. It was like a fairy-tale to them. But look at my neighbour over there greasing the wheels of his cart. Do you recognize him?"

"Is that the one who spoke of the coin?"

"I've seen his coin: 1721. He knows very well the year's seventeen and not just seven hundred. But now that he's heard the professor say that one can get a million for it, he is all in a daze thinking: 'Maybe it is seven hundred and I'll get my million for it.' He can't show it to the professor right here in the village because then everyone would know how rich he was: it has to be kept secret. That's why he's greasing his cart. He will go to town tomorrow to show the piece. I'm sure of it. Tomorrow isn't market day and there is nothing else he can go to town for. I know him well enough."

When I climbed up into the loft I found Lyova already asleep. He was muttering over and over again, "Norman, Norman."

Afraid that he was disturbing the professor, I woke him up and told him to lie down nearer me.

"Lyova, why did you keep saying, 'Norman, Norman'?" the professor asked.

"Oh, I have an idea, Alexander Andreyevich, but there may be nothing in it. You said that the thigh-bone we found was very long and that it must have belonged to a man. I wanted to ask you, is it too big for an ordinary man?"

"Yes, I think it is."

"Perhaps it was a Norman then? That's what I was thinking of. Could it have been a Norman?"

"No, Lyova. If he were a Norman we should have found an urn of ashes there, because the Normans cremated their dead."

Lyova went to sleep and muttered no more.

Thoughts of primitive man no longer kept me awake; I could visualize him easily now. We all slept soundly and woke in happy anticipation of going on with our excavation and journey.

We were lucky that day. The sun appeared and we soon located the belt which had escaped observation the day before. It was the layer of turf on which the mound had been built. We could also see the edge of the grave distinctly. We drew a line from east to west over the spot where the bone had been found and began to dig the reception trench to get at the skeleton. The main diggers again were Lyova and Pavel, while we lay on top of the mound watching. Lyova, who was now definitely in command, pitched into anybody careless enough to knock down a lump of earth with his elbow. Nikolai was with us, watching, spilling down earth more often than any of the others: he seemed on edge somehow, though he tried not to show it.

The proximity of the skeleton made it dangerous to go on digging with a spade. Pavel came up and lay down beside us, while the professor went below to show Lyova how to remove the earth by hand. Leaving him to it he climbed up.

"The skull will appear first," he said.

At this Nikolai knocked down a large lump of earth.

Lyova squeezed every crumb of earth between his fingers and showed the professor every tiny stone he came upon.

"This must be the skull," he would say whenever his finger touched something hard.

And Nikolai would invariably knock down a lump of earth.

"You must be scared, Nikolai," Lyova said. "Why don't you go?"

"The head! The head!" Lyova shouted suddenly, and it looked as though he was right this time.

The professor went below and examined the spot.

"Yes, it is," he said.

Nikolai grew pale, his eyes fastened on the spot.

"I suppose it's excavations like ours that will one day explain the origin of man," Pavel said softly.

Nobody said a word. We were all waiting excitedly to see what a man's skull would look like after some eight hundred years in the earth. It turned out to be more impressive than I had imagined. Its colour was not the colour of bone but almost that of copper or burnt clay. Face down it could have been mistaken for a small jug that gold is sometimes found in. Lyova scraped the earth from the facial part, revealing the forehead and teeth which were perfectly white.

When the teeth appeared amid our tense silence Nikolai suddenly guffawed, shrilling higher and higher like a siren or rather neighing like a young stallion. Reaching the highest pitch, he ended in an obscene oath.

This was the cry of the never changing ape deprived of the creative spirit. Though familiar, the sound seemed weird, disgusting, and above everything else inane. We looked up in surprise and then burst out laughing.

Pavel alone did not laugh. This was too personal for him to be funny. He looked at the neighing brother with his large, gray, thought-tormented eyes.

"Shut up, you fool!" he said as to an ape. "Such excavations tell us about the origin of man."

There were many peculiarities about the burial of this tall ancestor with the unusually white teeth. The position of some of the bones, especially those of the neck, seemed to be unnatural. But the professor made no comment. And only when we were out on the lake again he suggested, "Most likely he had been hanged."

THE SPRING OF MAN

The Appearance of the Mayfly

Two rivers, one flowing through the fertile fields of Opolye into the Oka, and the other through the swamps of Zalesye—the land of the Drevlyans*—into the Volga, for some reason bore the same name—Nerle. The river we followed from Lake Syomino was the Greater Nerle and the other one the Lesser Nerle. There was a portage between the two and both formed a continuous route between Zalesye and Opolye, and that is probably why they both bore the same name.

The route along the Greater Nerle was so tortuous through monotonous swamps that we seemed to be approaching the church of Kopnino village one minute and going away from it the next. A young shepherd was learning how to play his pipe somewhere on the bank, and the sound kept swelling and fading all day long.

Both Sergei Sergeyevich's glass and Father Filimon's leg pointed to rain, and rain it did from morning till night. But this was a season when every single day brings something of beauty. Towards evening, when the sun came out, especially lovely after its long absence, we saw sharp rocks jutting out of the water and a forest of pines on the high bank. Father Filimon asked our chief for permission to land for a few minutes. We all guessed what he wanted on that high bank. It would take time to get a complete picture of the country from our measurements of the river, the speed of the current, the readings of altitude, the population figures and their chief occupations, obtained from chairmen of the village Soviets, the areas of arable land and meadows, the drawings of the roofs of huts in the woods, the carved window-frames and weather-cocks. But Father Filya thought he had only to climb the high bank to discover a new country from end to end.

---

* The Drevlyans were an ancient Slavonic tribe populating dense forests.

Still, the spot commanded a view worth climbing for: high banks overgrown with pines so tall that if you bent back to look at their tops your hat would fall off, the river spangled with white and golden water-lilies, and green gates affording a glimpse of such vast back-waters that it was hard to tell which way the river went: the creek was much broader than the river itself and enticing to the traveller if not for the two green sentries, long slender reeds swaying in the current, showing where the river ran and which way to go.

The hardships of travelling are redeemed by moments of pure bliss when some insignificant detail suddenly reveals the splendour of the world. As we sat waiting for the priest's return we watched the ballet of mayflies over the water, beautiful in the slanting rays of the evening sun. Those white creatures, not unlike butterflies, had but one day to live—and how beautifully they lived this one day, their only one. It moved me because I, too, had a day like this to remember.

Suddenly from above, where a road ran through the pine forest, we heard a song as brief and light as the life of a mayfly and then another and a third sung by a chorus of girls' voices, and it seemed to us that this was the tune the mayflies were dancing to. Our Robin-sons got out their mandolin and balalaika in readiness. A cart full of village girls slowly emerged from the trees above. When they caught sight of our young men, the girls sang:

> *Darting glances quick and flashing*
> *My brown eyes are full of go.*
> *Lots of fellows young and dashing*
> *Fall for them, I'll have you know.*

The Robinsons waited for the girls above to draw level with their boat and then struck up their improvised reply:

> *I rowed my boat towards the shore*
> *And saw my darling from below.*
> *All dressed up but, oh, her legs*
> *Were slender like a pair of kegs!*

Squeals of laughter came from the girls, and just then Father Fili-mon, beaming all over, appeared with a handful of wild strawberries.

"Well, Father, what's the news up there? What's that you're carrying?"

"The climate must be milder in these parts," said Father Filimon.

"At Pereslavl the strawberries are just in flower, but here they are ripe already."

The Nettle Feast

The appearance of our armada in these desolate waters seemed short of a miracle to the natives, and a village in a body followed us along the bank to the next where more people joined in until finally the whole crowd met us as we landed. After staring their fill at us, some of them led me aside, showering me with questions. They were particularly curious about our priest.

"Is he a real priest?"

"Of course," I said. They exchanged glances.

"A real priest, you say?"

"Yes, of course."

That appeared remarkable to these people living so far from the railway. They swarmed around our tents all night, the more inquisitive lifting the flaps and keeping us awake.

Next day our ethnographical group set out for the village of Likhorevo to see the Nettle Feast which was probably a relic of the cult of Yarilo.

I had my doubts that we would witness any rites at all, and expected it would all boil down to jotting down a story told by some old woman. We did not ask about the ritual the moment we came, of course: ostensibly we were there to have a look at their pottery. It was only when the hearts of these potters were fully opened to us that we asked about the celebration of the feast that marks the climax of spring's re-creative powers, and about the heathen god. An old man of well over sixty came forward, smiling much like an old faun.

"It's me you want, truly and honestly," he said, showing his strong white teeth.

The potters then stopped talking about their craft and formed a cheerful ring around this priest of the God Yarilo.

"Vlasich will show you everything," everyone assured us.

"I'll try," said Vlasich.

Soon we heard singing and hurried into the open where the women and girls were *clearing the field*—in the usual way: the women approached the girls, singing:

That's how we cleared it, cleared it, cleared it!

Then the girls pressed towards the women, so that both groups moved slowly down the village street, enacting the old drama to the words of the ancient song: "We sowed the millet, the millet, the millet."

Some went through the motions of sowing, others pretended to let the horses trample the field, the neighbours chased the horses and captured them, demanding a young girl as ransom. A young man interceded for the girl and then came the fight.

The whole was a prelude—the field had now been cleared so that the sowing might begin without delay.

His long whispered discussion with the leading women over, Vlasich stood waiting for the field to be ready.

"He is our sowing man," somebody in the crowd said.

It was explained to us that the women had indeed chosen Vlasich long before to be their sower and no one else could do it for him. From time to time he would disappear somewhere, coming back ever more flushed and cheerful. At last he brought a huge pole about ten times as long as himself. A bundle of nettles was tied to one end.

He lifted the pole up.

> *Yarilo is here*
> *Sturdy as oak*
> *Tall as a pole.**

A wide ring of spectators was formed round the sower with the children sitting in three groups forming a triangle within it.

Marfa Baranova, a famous local fun organizer, took her place beside the old sower. She was the other leading character—the sower's old woman. Both grandad and grandma got busy arranging the children so that there would be more room to walk between them, and giving advice to the leaders of the women and girls about their intricate movements in the ring. At last everybody was ready and the first links of the chain of women dressed in their holiday finery entered the ring and snaked between the three groups of children while the rest wove in a spiral. They all actually trod the same path, but the children were soon hidden from view and the dancers seemed no longer to be moving at all but just swaying like a field of ripe rye

---

* "Yarilo" by Sergei Gorodetsky.—*Auth.*

towards the tall pole with the bunch of nettles on it and the old couple standing beneath.

The chorus sang:

> There's poppies on the hill
> And poppies down below,
> Fair poppies, dear girls,
> Stand in a row!

Then came the questions:

> Are the peas ripe?
> Are the beans ripe?
> Are the greens ripe?

The chorus fell silent, waiting for the old couple to answer.

No, the peas were not ripe. Why, the ground was not even ploughed yet, because there was no horse. The colt had to grow up first but even a colt they didn't have, some mare's eggs had to be sent for first.

The crowd laughed and the dancers began circling again and singing:

> The poppies on the hill—

Then the singers once more asked whether the peas were ripe and the old man answered that the colt had grown but there had been another misfortune: the plough was broken and they had had to ask the blacksmith to forge them a ploughshare six inches long.

They sang and danced, and then there was more trouble: the old man fell ill and there was no one to do the ploughing and sowing.

And so the old man was ailing and the girls were full of impatience, dancing and asking:

> Are the peas ripe?

They cheered up when the old man grew better and could even bandy a few jokes with his old woman, and what jokes they were! And the peas were doing very well too.

"Peas ought to be good," cried the sower.

There were the tendrils, there were the pods six inches long.

Then the whole crowd of women pressed forward and asked for the last time:

Are the peas ripe?
Are the beans ripe?
Are the greens ripe?

With a loud cry "They are!" grandad let go of the pole with its nettles; the women scattered as it crashed to the ground, the old man grabbed his old woman and the young men chased the girls swishing their legs with the stinging nettles.

The spectators enjoyed this tremendously and kept repeating:

They are ripe.

Vessels of Abomination

When the performance was over, we all met at Vlasich's house and sent for Marfa Baranova. We took down all the details of the ceremony with its many jokes the implications of which left no doubt whatever that we were indeed dealing with Yarilo, the god of spring in man. True, these were pitiful scraps of the old cult, yet the reverence, lost by the majority of people now, for the force that brings man into being could be resurrected from them, we could even see how this was achieved—everything was called almost by its gross name, but this grossness was essential, like the grossness of the earth itself producing the finest lacework of herb and flower.

We were content and even happy with these poor scraps of the spring of man because we were men of science, whose lot it is to be satisfied with mere scraps.

Our return journey was delayed just the way it was put in the Nettle Feast show: the colt was still in the field and had to be caught and brought to us. And so we sat talking with Vlasich and Marfa Baranova, but not for long. The room was soon filled with inquisitive villagers, and suddenly four women to whom we had given some money after their Nettle Feast performance rushed into the cottage as though swept by a hurricane, all shouting at once like a flock of great birds. Their Bacchantic onrush was uncanny; we were afraid they would pounce on us and tear us all to pieces. The woman whose face seemed hewn out of stone and painted all colours was the loudest; another one was sallow-skinned, the third was quite red in the face and the fourth was dark and pretty. Whirling in a frenzy of excitement they went on yelling, their teeth flashing in their open mouths. At last we

made out that they were all shouting the same two words "sixty kopeks." Their meaning dawned on us and when we gave one of them
the money, they all tore out of the house and down the street, some
of them stumbling as they ran.

"Widows and childless wives," Vlasich said by way of explanation.

"Widows—I can understand that," I said. "But the childless women
have their husbands."

"Can a man keep a childless wife in check? She is a free woman."

There could be no doubt we had seen those same stubborn heathens
whom our early Christian fathers had called the vessels of abomi-
nation.

But such women could be found in every village and there was
nothing remarkable about that. What struck us was the attitude of
those respectable peasants who sat in Vlasich's house.

"We think that these women are very useful," one of them said
quite bluntly. "Somebody has to cheer us up once in a while."

The Flowering of the Rye

The evening was calm and beautiful. The rye had begun to flower.
Everything breathed of nature's potent love, of growing living things
born of the earth. As we drove with Vlasich in his cart he told us
about himself. He had been out of luck with his first wife. To save
her, the child had to be dismembered in her womb and after that
she was no longer a proper wife to him. He had to bear with her for
years. Not that he had lived in celibacy, but he had no children and
a peasant's life is no good without them. His wife died at last, he
married a young woman, the children came along, but they were still
small while he was already over sixty, and his strength was ebbing,
though he had to work harder than ever to provide for a growing
family. He was afraid he would not live to see his sons take over his
cares.

We were passing through a village and noticed an unusually long
aerial. Vlasich showed great interest and we told him something about
radio.

"Have you heard about the monkey seeds?" he asked. "They give
you an injection, they say, and you're five years younger."

"Why five?" remarked my companion. "Better say twenty-five."

"No, no," said Vlasich. "Five years would do for me, just till my boys grow up. I don't want any more." And he very gravely begged us to help him get the "seeds."

The village where the aerial stood seemed endless. We went on and on but could not come to the end of it. It reached over the hill and down through the marshes and then climbed another hill—it was clear that the people were multiplying vigorously in this outlying spot.

And now, in the orange light of the last afterglow we saw the junction of the Nerle and Kubra rivers. Over the bridge lay another village, that of Grigorovo, as bursting with people as Andrianovo. There were crowds along the banks and in the streets, the whole place was teeming with life and resounding with snatches of songs, brief and light as the mayflies. Our Father Filya was gliding downstream in his boat with at least forty children aboard head to head like Grandad Mazai's hares.* He was giving them a ride. The Robinsons had the girls with them also packed as tightly as Mazai's hares, all singing to the mandolin and the balalaika. When the villagers caught sight of us, they followed our cart along the bank in a body as far as our camp on the bank of the Kubra. It had taken just that one day to make our expedition jump its scientific track, and when our Filya turned up, rather the worse for liquor, but as timid as ever in the presence of his learned chief, he received this admonition: "Don't overdo your nature studies, Father."

---

* A reference to a story about an old peasant who saved the hares stranded by the spring floods. The passage from Nekrasov's poem is well known from the children's *Readers*.

SUMMER

SUMMER

The First Pointing

My pointer pup was named Romulus, but I called him simply Roma or Romka, and sometimes, more formally, Roman Vasilyevich. The parts of him that grew fastest were his ears and paws. His ears in fact were so long that they fell over his eyes when he looked down, while his legs were constantly tripping him up.

Here is what happened today: he was scrambling up the cellar stairs when his clumsy paw loosened a brick which went bumping down into the cellar. Much surprised by this, Roma stood cocking his head first to one side then to the other to free his eyes from those flapping ears.

"What d'you make of that, Roman Vasilyevich!" I said. "That brick bouncing down there looks quite alive, doesn't it?"

Roma eyed me intelligently.

"Stop goggling! Mind that thing down there doesn't pluck up courage and come bouncing back to punch you on the nose."

Roma shifted his eyes. He was evidently tingling to run down and see why that ordinary dead brick had suddenly come to life. But then again, to go down there was not altogether safe. What if the brick got hold of him and pulled him down into the dark cellar for ever and ever?

"What shall we do then?" I asked. "Cut and run, eh?"

Roma's glance was fleeting, but I caught his meaning.

"That's just what I've been thinking. But what if I turn and he catches me by the tail?"

So this was no good either, and Roma stood still for a long time doing the first point in his life at an inanimate brick—just like an adult dog when it scents game in the grass.

The longer he stood there, the more frightened and apprehensive he became: according to canine logic the deader an enemy plays the more terrible his final spring.

"I'll outwit him," Roma said to himself. But he fancied the brick was whispering, "I'll outlie him!"

A brick will think nothing of lying still for hundreds of years if need be, but it's hard on a poor little puppy: he grew so tired he shivered all over.

"What shall we do, Roman Vasilyevich?" I asked.

"Should I try a bark?" he asked in his own way.

"Why not?"

Roma barked and leapt back, imagining that he had awakened the brick and it had stirred. Keeping a safe distance he watched to see if the thing was not climbing out of the cellar after him. Now he stole back warily and peeped down.

"Perhaps I should try another one?"

He barked and sprang back again.

This time, his bark brought Kate, his mother, to the scene. Glaring at the spot he was barking at she began to descend slowly, step by step. Romka stopped barking of course, trusting that the matter was now in safe paws, and looked on more boldly.

Kate scented Roma's print on the dreaded brick and sniffed at it. The thing was quite dead and harmless. To be on the safe side though, she sniffed at everything, but finding nothing suspicious, looked up and said to Roma with her eyes:

"I think there's nothing to be afraid of, son."

Romulus brightened up and wagged his tail. When Kate turned to go he ran after her and began to worry her by the ear.

The School in the Bushes

A young pointer must be taught to keep within range of the gun, that is, fifty paces, and even closer if it's forest country. The most important thing though is to teach the pup to be constantly aware of its master and not get carried away by any adventures of its own. All this put together—ranging through the fields in circles and keeping sight of the master in forest country—is called good initial training.

I went for a walk up a wooded hill and took Romka along. This place is called the "allotment" because it has been allotted to the people of the nearby townlet for firewood. It has all been divided into lots and each man cuts as much wood as he needs from his own private plot. Some cut none at all and their plots stand out like densely overgrown islands, others fell the taller trees leaving the saplings to grow, and there are some who clean out their plots completely, leaving nothing but a heap of rotting twigs. As a result, the hill looked like the head of a man who had been given a haircut by a blind barber.

I could hardly expect to find game in a spot so near town. But this was all the better for the first stage in training. The dog would be learning one thing at a time: ranging properly, and keeping his master ever in mind.

I unfastened the leash and stroked Romka. He did not notice I had set him free and stood by me as before.

"Search," I said, waving my hand.

He understood and tore away. In a second he was in the bushes, but, losing sight of me, he got frightened and came back. For a few moments he stood perfectly still and looked at me in a very peculiar manner—as though he were photographing me to carry my likeness with him into the bushes and among the tree-stumps, so unlike humans in shape. Finished with this mysterious process, he wagged his tail and was gone.

There is a world of difference between woods and fields where the dog is always in sight. In the woods, the dog which has vanished on the left has to be taught to make an invisible circle and appear on your right, and so keep circling like a top. If it does not show up on the right it can only mean that it has scented game somewhere and is pointing. You can watch your dog best when walking along a path in the wood because it keeps crossing back across it.

But my Romka vanished in a thicket and did not come back. I was glad that his sense of freedom proved stronger than his attachment to his master. I did not mind: I am a sportsman and like my freedom, too. But I had to teach him to use his freedom in co-ordination with me, to satisfy both of us. I crossed to another cleared plot taking long leaps through the shrubbery to avoid leaving enough tracks to make finding me too easy. In the center of the clearing I saw a large clump of junipers and took a running jump right into the middle of it.

I could not hear the pattering of the dog's feet on the wet grass, but I did hear the snapping of twigs and his loud panting. He must have suddenly realized I wasn't there and dashed about looking for me getting badly out of breath in his excitement. He guessed my whereabouts fairly accurately though, since he came tearing into the clearing from which I had made my leap.

When the noise stopped I gave a sharp whistle. It was very much like a game of blind man's buff.

My whistle must have reached him just as he stopped to listen and puzzle things out. He sensed correctly the direction of the sound and made a frantic dash puffing like a steam engine. He stopped short at the edge of the clearing where I crouched motionless in the bushes.

What with his hard run and fright, he was exhausted and his tongue lolled. He could not scent anything in this condition of course, and had to depend on his ears alone. He pricked up his ears but they wouldn't stay erect, the ends drooped and obstructed his hearing. He tried cocking his head to one side—no good, to the other—no good either. He saw what the trouble was, at last: he could not hear his master's signal because of his own breathing. He snapped his mouth shut, but in his haste bit a lip and so stood listening with one lip thrust over the other.

I was choking with laughter looking at his funny face and had to clamp my hand over my mouth. But he did not hear me. The woods without his master were a wilderness where only the wolves, his fore-bears, were prowling. They would never forgive him for betraying their cause, for his devotion to man, for his snug cubby-hole and security—they would tear him to pieces and devour him. When one lives with the wolves one must howl like one, says an old proverb.

And he tried it. He lifted up his head and howled.

I had never heard him howl like this before. He had actually sensed the wilds and was howling as young wolves do when their mother goes out after prey and is long in coming back.

For this is what might have happened. She had killed a lamb and while carrying it to her family was tracked down and waylaid by a hunter. Man found and took her cubs and fed them. The fount of tenderness in nature's creatures is inexhaustible: the young wolves transferred their affection to the man who had adopted them, licking his hands, leaping about and putting their paws on his chest. They never knew that it was he who had killed their mother. But the wild wolves did and were the deadly enemies of both man and the one who had betrayed their cause, the dog.

Romka was howling so pitifully that I was really sorry for him. But pity I could not afford, for I was the teacher; and so I remained still, holding my breath.

He turned his back to me and listened in another direction. Was it a sandpiper whistling somewhere in the sky? Or was it his master calling him from up there?

Somewhere in a nearby field a cow must have frightened a lapwing who whistled as he whirred up. This was not so high or far away and surely must be the master! Romka rushed to this sound, but then I whistled sharply: "Here I am."

He came back. In a space of fifteen minutes I had worn him out, shown him how frightening a lonely forest was without humans, and had struck terror in his heart that would last for the rest of his life, a terror of the wolves, his forebears. When at last I purposely stirred in the bushes and lit my pipe, he caught a whiff of my tobacco and knew me at once. His ears lay flat, his head became as smooth and round as a water-melon. When I stood up, he lay down shamefacedly. I came out of the clump, stroked him, and he began leaping about rapturously, barking madly.

Yarik

I had lost my pointer and for some time I had to do my shooting "by tracks," that is, by finding the tracks of birds in the morning dew and following them like a dog. I cannot say for sure but I believe I could pick up the scent at times too.

About this time, a vet who lived thirty versts or so away had mated his marvelous Irish setter bitch with a dog of the same breed. They both came from the same place—a former landowner's estate. And just when I was finding things especially hard my friend presented me with a six-week-old Irish setter. I accepted the gift very gratefully and reared the pup to be a real friend. Training a dog gave me just as much pleasure as shooting game.

I remember one day in a clearing dotted with old black tree-stumps. There was a profusion of red flowers shaped like fir saplings. They made the whole clearing look red though there were plenty of wild pansies there, half blue and half yellow, and many daisies with yellow buttons, and bluebells, and lilac lady's smock—all the flowers you could imagine. And yet the fir-like flowers made the whole clearing look red. You could still find some wild strawberries, overripe and very sweet, near the old black tree-stumps. A bit of rain in the summer did not matter really. I sat it out under one of the firs, and blew smoke rings at the gnats to keep them from worrying my dog Yarik.

When that did not help, I kindled a small fire of fir cones which soon drove the gnats out into the rain. No sooner had we vanquished them than the rain stopped. A summer shower gives you nothing but pleasure.

We had to sit under the tree for half an hour longer anyway, waiting for the birds to begin feeding and leave their fresh prints on the ground. When I thought time was up I came out into the red clearing and unleashed Yarik.

"Go to it, my friend," I said.

Yarik was in his third summer of training, the senior and final grade for Irish setters. If all went well I would have the finest gun-dog in the world towards the end of the summer, an Irish setter of my own training, tireless and with an amazingly long-range scent.

I often looked at my Yarik's nose enviously thinking to myself: Wouldn't I run against the wind over the flowering clearing, catching the most delightful smells if only I had a scent like that!

But we have no sense of smell to speak of, and are deprived of a great deal of pleasure. We always ask: Is your sight good? Do you hear well? But nobody ever asks: How is your sense of smell? Is your nose good? I have been training dogs for years, and whenever a dog scents game and leads me, I am always excited, thinking: If I could only have sensed the game myself!

"Well, go to it, citizen," I repeated.

And he began circling the red clearing.

He soon stopped at the edge under the trees, sniffed hard and turned, slanting his eyes at me very gravely, as though inviting me to follow: no words were necessary. He led me very slowly, crouching a little like a fox.

We got to a thick clump of bushes which only Yarik could squeeze into. But I was not going to let him go on alone, afraid that he might plunge after the birds wet from the rain and undo the whole course of his training. I was just going to call him back when he suddenly waved his splendid wing of a tail and glanced at me. I understood.

"They spent the night in there but have been feeding in the red clearing."

"What shall we do?" I asked.

He sniffed at the flowers but the shower had washed away the tracks except for those we had followed under the trees.

The only thing to do was to describe a new circle and find the fresh tracks made after the rain. But he had not covered half of it when he stopped still near a small but thick clump of bushes. The whiff he caught was so overpowering that he froze in a very strange attitude: his body twisted almost into a horse-shoe, so that he could have easily admired his own tail. I went up and stroked him.

"Go on if you can."

He straightened and stepped forward. It was possible to go on, but very cautiously. After walking round the bush gingerly, he told me in his own way:

"They were here during the rain."

He led me on, the fluffy end of his tail almost trailing, following the fresh tracks which could be detected with the naked eye—a green trail against the grass, grey with the raindrops.

The birds had probably sensed our approach and were hurrying away. Yarik explained it to me.

"They're just ahead of us and very near too."

They all got into a large clump of juniper and Yarik made his final, *dead* point. Until then he had been free to pant from time to time, lolling his tongue, but now his jaws were set with only the tip of his pink tongue showing like a tiny petal, for it was too late to draw it in. A gnat settled on it swelling with blood, and I could see how Yarik's brown leather button of a nose quivered with both pain and scent, but he could not pull his tongue in now because the sound might frighten the birds.

Not nearly as excited as Yarik, I went up to him cautiously, and flicked away the gnat. Yarik looked splendid. He stood as if turned to stone, his gorgeous tail in a line with his rigid back, while his eyes were alive and blazing with eagerness.

Noiselessly I moved round the clump till I stood opposite Yarik to make the bird fly straight up instead of escaping in my direction. We stood like that for quite a long time, and the birds were certainly aware that they were surrounded. I stepped towards the bush and heard the hen saying to her children:

"I'll go and have a look, and you wait for me here."

And out she flew with a terrific whirr.

If she had flown towards me Yarik would not have budged. Nor would he have even if she had flown over him, remembering as he would what a crime it was to chase a flushed bird when the real quarry was still in the bushes. But the huge grey hen, almost the size of a domestic fowl, somersaulted in the air, practically winged the dog's nose, and then fluttered very low, taunting him with her cry:

"Why don't you catch me. Don't you see I can't fly?"

About ten paces away she dropped to the ground like a stone and scurried through the red flowers. This was too much for Yarik, and forgetting his years of training, he rushed after her.

And so her ruse was a success. She had decoyed the enemy from her brood, and up she went crying to her young in the bushes, "Scatter away, fly off, all of you!"

The young birds flew out of the juniper in every direction, piping as they went:

"You darned fool!"

"Come back," I shouted to my duped friend. He came to his senses at once and trudged back to me guiltily.

"What have you done?" I asked in a studiously fearful voice.

He lay down.

"Come, come now!"

He laid his head on my knee, asking to be forgiven.

"All right," I said, and squeezed into the juniper clump. "Come here, sit still and don't pant. We'll make fools of them yet."

Some ten minutes later, I whistled softly, imitating a young grouse: "Phew-phew," which means, "Where are you, ma?"

"Quokh, quokh," she replied, meaning, "Coming."

We heard more calls just like mine: "Where are you, ma?" "Coming," she answered them all.

One of the young birds peeped quite closely and I kept replying until it ran up so near that I could see the grass ripple right under my knee. Looking Yarik straight in the eye and shaking my fist at him, I swiftly covered the spot with the palm of my hand and pulled out a grey bird about the size of a pigeon.

"Smell it," I said softly.

Yarik turned his head away, afraid to open his mouth and pant.

"Come on, smell it, my dear fellow," I pleaded, "come on!"

He sniffed and puffed like a steam engine.

That was the hardest punishment I could think of.

Now I whistled quite boldly, certain that the mother would come running when she found one of her chicks missing. There were seven others and I heard them fall silent one by one as each found its mother. When all of them were quiet, I acted as the eighth and whistled softly: "Where are you, ma?"

"Come here," she replied.

"Phew-phew, I cannot. You'd better bring them all to me."

And sure enough, I saw her running towards us through the grass, her neck popping up now and then like a green bottle-neck, with her brood stirring the grass in her wake. They all settled down a few paces off.

"Now, don't play the fool a second time," I said to Yarik with a look, and let my chick go. It fluttered up and the whole family of them flew up and away, while we watched them, laughing.

"That's how we made fools of you, good citizens!"

Verny

I had trained Yarik very well for the marshes, but with my passion for shooting in the wood, I could not resist taking him with me after black grouse. That was a mistake. I should have waited another season. In the first days, however, Yarik did very well, as well as in the marshes, except that I had to whistle to him more often. But as we were coming home one evening, a grey hen with a belatedly hatched brood crossed our path and began to tease Yarik with her usual tricks. He rushed after her, stumbled on the chicks and lost his head completely, dashing madly back and forth. I lost my temper and gave him such a thrashing that he ran off. I started after him, but he got away and stayed out all night. Next morning I saw his ginger ears showing in the potato patch.

Those who have ever trained dogs will understand my despair: it would take a lot of hard work to set the dog aright now, and taking him out again that season was absolutely out of the question. There was only one thing to do—find another dog and train Yarik again from the very beginning so that the incident could gradually fade from his memory.

I began to look about for another dog, something like my late Fleita even, so long as I could do some shooting with it.

I made inquiries everywhere and sent my boys out scouting. One day they came back and told me that as they were passing a farmstead with many beehives in the orchard, they saw an old man come out of the house with an axe in his hand and start chopping wood. When he had done quite a lot, the old man whistled and a dog appeared: black with ginger spots, very shaggy and clearly a thoroughbred. The dog took the splitting of a log in its teeth, carried it indoors, came back and took another, in short, it carried the whole lot in while its master sat resting. The old man then locked his front door, brought some more wood out of the shed, chopped it up too, and let the dog

carry it back into the shed piece by piece. The boys had run home
without waiting to see it out, but it was obvious from the size of the
stack that the old man must have been doing this day after day,
providing fuel against the winter or perhaps for sale.

"Are you sure the dog was black with ginger spots and a very thick
coat?" I asked.

"Of course," said the boys. "Its forehead is even rounder than our
Yarik's and the muzzle seemed to have a dent. It was so shaggy, it
looked like a caveman."

Next day I went there to try my luck and found everything just as
the boys had described it: the old man chopping wood and a fine
Gordon setter carrying it into the shed. On one trip the dog, tired
out, dropped its burden midway and came back. The old man picked
up a stick. The dog came to him and lay right at his feet. The old
man gave it two savage blows and threw the stick aside. The dog
jumped up, picked up the stick, made several leaps around its master,
returned to the chunk it had dropped, carried it to the shed, and
went on with its work briskly.

The dog had a most striking head, much like a Louis XIV wig, but
its hind parts were stiff and clumsy either from too many beatings
or from distemper. People told me afterwards about the beatings the
dog had suffered while doing the woodman's job: it was quite likely
that this was the cause.

"Why do you put a good gun-dog to this kind of work?" I asked.

"Some gun-dog that," muttered the old man. "I can't even train
him to stack the wood properly. He brings it in all right, but always
throws it down any old way."

The old man's son had heard us talking and came out to see who
was there. The samovar was kindled and I was invited in. As we sat
drinking tea, I told them about my trouble with Yarik and said I
would not mind buying their Verny, as the dog was called, if its scent
were any good at all. They told me they had bought the dog from a
man named Bendrishev during the famine more out of pity for the
man than anything else. He had praised the dog highly. I knew
Bendrishev, he was one of our finest wildfowlers and trainers, and
it occurred to me that these peasants simply had no idea what a dog
like that was worth. I thought I should take the chance and buy the
dog then and there before they got wise to it. When I asked what
they wanted for him they suggested twenty rubles—a mere trifle. But
it would never do to let a peasant feel his price was too low, and so
I began to haggle furiously. There we sat drinking tea and eating

honey, haggling our heads off, though I would have gladly offered them thirty instead of the twenty they wanted. My hosts also drank one cup of tea after another, sweating and haggling. The funniest thing was that it was not the dog they were praising but its former master, repeating that Bendrishev knew his hunting as Father Yegor knew the Lord's Prayer. Finally, I struck a bargain, gaining in addition fifteen pounds of honey and a whistle, and made for home as fast as I could make it.

I kept Verny indoors for two days making friends with him until he became so attached to me that I only had to walk out of the room for him to start whining and whimpering. He was a very trusting, good-natured creature, brimming with orphan-like tenderness. On the third day, confident that he would never leave me now, I set out for the woods with my boys.

I had my Yarik for the marshes. I wanted to try Verny in the woods. As I released him in a clearing where we were likely to come across a brood of black grouse, he rushed into the bushes, but came back as if he had forgotten something and stood fixing us with his eye, cocking his shaggy head now to one side now to the other, as though he were an artist and we his models. He did it with a concentrated and businesslike air, then disappeared again, returned, and went on ranging about as a properly trained dog should in the woods. He caught a scent very soon where the clearing descended to the swamp edged with a thick patch of brushwood. He showed none of Yarik's excitement, no blazing eagerness in his eyes that could make a man forget he was a man and not a dog himself. He did his work very carefully as if only to oblige us, not to enjoy himself at all. He perhaps took too long over it and the distance between him and the birds increased. But soon he realized his mistake, stopped, looked around, made an unhurried circle and cut off the escape of the birds—doing everything casually, without a trace of excitement. We took up our positions in a line, with me in the middle and my boys on either side. Then I gave the order: "Go!"

The dog took a step forward, another step, then a bird whirred up, a shot rang, another bird—a shot again. We kept shooting and the birds fell into the marsh overgrown with reeds as tall as a man. Verny waited until the shooting was over, asked for permission with his eyes, went in himself, and brought them all out.

There was plenty of game in these parts, and within a few days we bagged enough of it to all but cover the cost of the new dog. People do strange things when good fortune goes to their heads. I wrote to

Verny's old owners and said I was greatly pleased with the dog and could not thank them enough, and that I quite agreed with them that Bendrishev knew his job as Father Yegor did his Lord's Prayer. Later I learned that my letter had simply crushed them: they had been sure the dog was no good and that Bendrishev had cheated them.

Verny had only been with us for no more than a few days when Yarik became a different dog. He was too proud to show he resented Verny. Even when I took my gun and Verny was leaping around, Yarik lay as still as a millstone, nothing in him betraying his yearning to go with us. Yet he was obviously suffering deeply and I had only to utter his name once for him to jump up and push Verny away. He had always been very careless about his food, gnawing at the easy parts of his bone and giving it up when it came to the tougher, less succulent bits. But now, afraid that Verny would get it, he guarded his bone and snarled if the other dog came near. When I called him he came to me, bone in mouth, and when he had a need to go outside he took his bone with him. Day after day Yarik provoked Verny to start a fight; this alarmed and worried me because I knew what these good-natured orphan-like dogs were like: they could stand a good deal but once their patience snapped they fought to a finish.

One washing day a tub with blueing water was left standing in the yard. Yarik lay gnawing at his bone nearby, and when it was almost picked clean he hid it under the tub. A few minutes later I called for Verny to come to the woods with me. Yarik was, of course, cut to the quick, but never turned a hair, nursing his grudge in secret. No need to say that an animal as clever as Yarik knew perfectly well that a dog called to go hunting cared nothing for a wretched bone. Verny happened to run past the tub where the bone was hidden and Yarik had a good excuse to attack him without revealing his jealousy. He pounced on him so furiously and deftly that Verny, badly handicapped by his stiff hind legs, fell backwards into the blueing water like an upset wooden horse. The way I saw it, Verny did not feel it particularly mortifying to lie in a tub of blueing water feet up for a moment, nor appear all wet and bedraggled before his master, after all the beatings and humiliations he had suffered during his wood-carrying days. It didn't hurt either. What did hurt was that he had done no wrong, he had not wanted that stupid bone at all—why then had this ginger gentleman gone for him like that? Was it not high time to put an end to it? He was ten times stronger too. And so out he jumped and went straight for Yarik.

Usually, when the odds are very uneven, the weaker dog will lie on the ground his belly up, while the stronger one stands over him merely snarling. After holding the loser in this position for a while, the winner trots to the nearest post or tree and leaves a note, probably the terms of a truce agreement. The loser then reads the note and leaves his own, very likely just endorsing it. I only rarely saw the loser add some reservation, but when this happened the winner presented a fresh note and acceptance of terms was signed to by the other party.

But no one as arrogant as Yarik could be expected to turn belly upwards—and sure enough, he rushed at his enemy and acquitted himself quite well at first.

Fearing for Yarik I lifted the tub and poured the blueing over the two snarling muzzles but it didn't help any. I then caught Verny by the tail and kicked Yarik in the chest, trying to pull the bigger dog away, but Yarik lunged for him more furiously than ever. I grabbed Yarik by the tail and pulled—which was worse still, for Verny sank his teeth into his throat and would have put an end to him in another minute. At that critical moment my boys came running out and pulled the dogs apart by their tails.

True to his nature, Verny bore no malice, but Yarik no longer bothered to conceal his hatred, and life in our yard became absolutely impossible. We tried to keep them apart, but we couldn't watch them all the time, so none of us felt easy in our minds.

One day in September when I was sure that we could stumble on no grouse broods in the wood I went out to have another try with Yarik. It was a complete success. Overjoyed with the triumph of my method of correcting one dog by working steadily and calmly with another, or simply because it was warm and I was tired, I forgot all about Verny when we came back and left Yarik out in the yard.

As we were having our dinner we heard an ominous growling outside and, looking out, saw the two mortal enemies slowly closing in, their hair bristling.

If we moved or made the slightest sound they would fall on each other at once, and so we sat holding our breath, hoping that it would blow over somehow, considering Yarik's satisfaction with the day's outing, and Verny being a good-natured dog anyway.

His hair on end, Yarik approached Verny, who was waiting gloomily for the next move. Yarik made a circle round the other dog, then went over to the wall and left his first note—possibly an overture for truce. Verny went up behind Yarik and sniffed at the root of his tail. After reading the note on the wall, he added his corrections in a

similar manner, while Yarik in turn sniffed at the root of his tail.
Yarik signed the document after which Verny made another half
circle and signed it once again, which probably denoted ratification
of the treaty.

We had peace in the yard after that. The dogs' duties were strictly
divided: Verny went mostly to the woods to track down black grouse,
to bell-shoot white partridges and the fat autumn woodcock on drier
land, while Yarik specialized in the marshes, going after common
and double snipe, and after grey partridges in the open fields. In the
woods I could depend on him only in the clearings, sparse shrubbery,
glades and on the forest edge.

Kate

Her parents were both prize-winners, well known to connoisseurs.
Her breed was the modern continental pointer. Her coat was white-
and-brown: two saddle-like brown patches on the back and brown
spots like so many coffee grains scattered all over the white.

It was I who had changed her name to Kate. Her former owners
had called her Kitty. They were a young married couple, gentle-
educated people. No children were born to them in the first two years
of marriage, and so they had babied Kitty. She had spent the two
years lolling on their sofa in Moscow, and in another month or two
this pedigree would have turned into a useless lap-dog. But towards
the end of the second year, the young wife began to find it hard to
climb the five flights of stairs to give the dog an airing while her
husband was away at the office. It was just about this time that my
Verny met disaster. He was bitten by a rabid dog. I shall not describe
how I had to part with him, the memory is too painful. When I heard
about the pointer I decided to try my luck with the dog, since I was
not quite happy with my hot-headed Yarik. I got the young couple
to sell me their dog, and they let me have it at a very fair price,
weeping a little at parting and begging me not to beat her.

I had heard from experienced trainers that it was not too late to
start training a dog at two so long as it had not been spoiled by some
bungling amateur. Kate was indeed so unspoiled that she never even
chased birds, but only went for flowers, biting off the heads of daisies
and tossing them high into the air. She had all the good qualities of
her breed—exceptionally good manners and intelligence. The fact
that she was a female was good too, bitches are quicker. As far as

indoor training went I broke her in in little more than a day. I put a bit of bread on the floor and when she tried to snap it up I cried, "No" and slapped her on the nose.

"Forget your sofa-lolling, dear lady."

In a quarter of an hour she no longer snapped up bread without permission, even if the piece were laid on her nose.

Next, I taught her to respond to the words "go," "back," "fetch," "here," "steady" and "to my side." The following day I took her out into the thick hazel undergrowth where there was no game. I would hide in the bushes and let her find me, so that in one day we went through the whole course of short wood-tracking. In the field, of course, it was somewhat more difficult. I would go forward like a yacht tacking against the wind, making her do the same by gestures or whistling. After three days of this, we were ready for training with game.

I took Kate into the marshes when the woodcock and snipe had not yet left the woods and there were only lapwings about. The manuals are entirely wrong, saying that lapwing is of not much use in training a dog. I, for one, think it is the best thing. True, full-grown lapwings are apt to over-excite a hot-headed young dog, but it is easy to scare them off with a few shots, and the chicks will lie as still as little ginger cakes, so one can all but tread on them.

Kate at first took no notice of the little cakes until I kicked one of them and it turned into a lapwing; too young to fly, it waddled off between the hummocks. I kept the dog still with the order "down," but allowed her to follow the bird with her eyes until it settled again between the hummocks, just another ginger cake.

"Steady! Go!"

She moved ahead crouching low. She did not point at all but just sniffed at it and the lapwing waddled on. I turned her head the other way to prevent her from seeing where the bird had settled, but made a note of it myself, and then set her to find it again by tacking against the wind.

She could not catch the scent in the air, but got a whiff from the tracks and wove her way, nose down, until she found the bird. Yet again she did not point but merely nudged the bird with her nose. We repeated this dozens of times but with the same result. She could not get the scent in the air and did no pointing. As I walked home I wondered if her two years spent indoors in Moscow had blunted her natural scent. However, perhaps it would come to life again in the new environment.

The marshes where we had trained with the lapwings were eight versts away. I could not go there very often just to see whether the snipe and double snipe had come into the open. But I found a marshy strip of about five acres much nearer. Kate flushed two full-grown snipe here and I used these for her daily training. But even this walk took two hours of my morning, and I always had to change completely afterwards because the way to that strip was very boggy. It was all the more annoying because I got no results. Kate would potter about in the marshes scaring the birds without doing herself any good at all.

One day I took my gun along and shot one of the two snipe. It dropped in a thicket. Kate found it, but in exactly the same way as she had found the lapwings: she kept circling round until she stumbled on it. This did her some good anyway in that she got to know the bird's scent, and I could hope for more progress the next day.

The throes of creative passion are not the poet's lot alone. There is no less torment in dog training, and just as with the poet, a bright idea may occur in the dead of night, starting you on a new track. As I lay awake I remembered a discussion in the columns of the *Huntsman* on the habits of snipe. Some contributors claimed that the male took no part in family life after mating, while others said that the cock was often found near the nest. And it struck me that since one of our two snipe was a cock and the other a hen, the nest could not be far away. In the morning I set off for the marsh with pleasurable anticipation. Kate pottered about as usual. One of the birds flew up and she did not budge. I parted the reeds and found four eggs on the hummock, surprisingly large for this small bird.

This really was a good find. I could now train Kate every day by leading her up to the nest on the leash and gradually developing her sense of scent. When the young birds hatched, she would search for them, and then I would hide them again and so on.

I was impatient to go there the next day, but the consequences were quite unexpected. The nest was about two hundred paces away from the edge of the marsh. When Kate had emerged from the bushes and gone no more than fifty paces, she halted and made her first point though we were still a good hundred and fifty paces off. Then she led the way, and, oh, so gracefully and expertly, pat-patting on with her slim legs like a ballet dancer. I was wearing huge top-boots, so big indeed that I had had to wrap a houseful of rags round my feet to make them stay on. She was pattering on with no more noise than drops of rain falling in the water, while I came crashing through like a mammoth. She even stopped, looked at me sternly and all but said:

"Quiet, for God's sake!"

At about five paces she made a final point and refused to move in spite of all my entreaties. And she was right, too, because as soon as I pulled a boot out of the mud with a loud squelch, up flew the bird.

Kate looked startled: "Oh dear, now you've done it!"

Still she did not move. I allowed her to go on and sniff cautiously at the nest. I was truly happy, but coming out of the marshes I noticed that they had already begun to mow the grass in the clearings and was told that our stretch of marsh would be done by evening. There was no use asking the peasants to mind the nest, there would certainly be one among them who would destroy it out of sheer contrariness. I went back into the marsh, cut some willow twigs and stuck them round the nest to make it look like a bush. The only thing I was afraid of, was that the hen would take fright and abandon the nest. But no, the very next day Kate led me through the mowed grass just as before, stopped about five paces away from my artificial bush, and the bird flew out again as before.

At this time the artist Boris Ivanovich and Mikhail Ivanovich, a doctor I knew, were also training their dogs elsewhere in the woods. The artist had a French pointer, and the doctor an Irish setter bitch. I invited them both ostensibly to have a chat over a cup of tea but my real object was to take them out into the marsh afterwards and show off a bit.

In a word, I was blowing my own trumpet, and was so happy that I even felt embarrassed and tried to say something nice to them.

"It was very wise of you, Boris Ivanovich, to choose a pointer," I said to the artist. "Look at mine, I've trained her in three weeks."

"It was very wise of you, Mikhail Ivanovich, to pick an Irish setter," I assured the doctor. "It means hard work, of course, but you'll have a dog to be proud of."

Needless to say, they were not slow in spreading abroad my unusual abilities in training gun-dogs, and I became a celebrity of sorts for miles around.

Never trust to sudden happiness, you young dog fanciers, sportsmen, newlyweds and poets. It is, indeed, an illusion and the highest hurdle in your path, which you must leap over and never rest on. My delight in my pedigree Kate's ideal pointing lasted no more than a week.

About a week after the hay had been cut in our marshy clearing, it looked even more lush than before. The day was gentle and grey and the clearing was so alluring, one felt it was crammed with snipe. And sure enough, one of them was scared up as soon as Kate made her first step. To my surprise, she never turned a hair. Then quite a young bird flew right up from under her paws, but she paid no attention whatever—she was leading to that same nest like one possessed. Then another young bird flew up and a third, a fourth, a fifth, but she kept leading straight on just as before, and exactly five paces from the nest pointed and froze in her posture. When I went over to have a look, I found nothing but egg-shells.

Thinking that the nest may have a stronger smell than the birds, I threw the shells away.

On the next day she led me to the nest again.

I destroyed the hummock, put some dry twigs in its place, and made a fire. Ignoring the young birds, she stumbled on, she led me to the burnt-out spot.

That meant that from the very start she had been working solely from memory. She was just acting. She could not feel life, she could just picture it. This dog was neither a sportsman's friend and helpmate nor the future mother of keen-scented puppies. She was an actress.

The usual thing to do in such cases is to shoot the dog. I decided to try and persuade her former owners to take her back, hinting casually at the usual fate of such dogs.

The next day brought the opening of the season and I joined the boys in their duck shoot though it was not really my sport. A week later I went out shooting young black grouse, which I like, but not overmuch either. I like shooting the latest grouse when the dog points far away from the bird and you have to use your own judgment to find the best position to meet their flight. One bird bagged at such a time is worth ten shot in summer.

The ash-berries were reddening. The martins had long gone, and the swallows too were gathering in flocks. The oats had been harvested. The lime-trees were yellow from top to bottom as were the willows and birches in the marshes. There had already been two light frosts and the potato stalks had turned black. The hunstman's heart was torn between many desires: there were the fascinating black grouse in the woods, the fat snipe in the marshes and the grey partridge in the fields. I tried to be everywhere and have a taste of everything, but then came the day when I was told, "Boris Ivanovich bagged a migrating double snipe yesterday."

Both grouse and partridge were forgotten and I walked eight versts to the Lyakhovo marshes to watch for the migrating flocks. And if I shot two birds one day and three the next, I thought I was doing fine.

Just as I was doing my finest my feet got so blistered by my beastly boots that I could not walk to the marshes any more. Hiring a horse at harvest time is too expensive, but what really held me back was that I'd be ashamed to: I simply can't bring myself to drive a-shooting.

It was a wistful sort of day. The nests in the tall birch-trees looked like old gold. Kate came up to me so sad and miserable. How thin she had been getting lately.

I felt sorry for the pretty thing. We had plenty of grey partridge in the stubble behind our house and I never shot them as game just because they were so close. But why not try the dog on them, and shoot one or two for the pot?

I went out in my sandals. The wind happened to be blowing our way, and I set Kate off tacking against it. At one of the very first tacks she sniffed the air, jumped aside and halted in her tracks. Then she leaped to the other side, as graceful as a ballet dancer and halted again, her eyes fastened on the same spot. And so she went on slicing the space between me and the unseen point like a piece of cheese until she found herself near her goal and headed on, just as she had done with the empty nest.

She finally made a point quivering like a throbbing motor, making a supreme effort not to leap into the heart of the scent.

And then suddenly—have you ever heard the frightful whirr a flock of grey partridge makes when thirty of them or more are flushed up? I shot one and then another, and both birds fell a little distance away.

She saw them drop.

Then I understood. I had been training her in a wooded swamp hemmed in by bushes, where the air was quite still. There she had been unable to understand what was required of her, and had just pottered about with her nose to the ground. But in an open place like this the strong wind had immediately roused her sense of smell, which had been blunted in town.

Once she had got the hang of it with the partridge she was sure to do it with the snipe and double snipe in the open marshes. I had quite forgotten that I was in my sandals and carried no food with me. How could I think of it now? I covered the eight versts to the marshes almost at a run.

I gave her the try-out first in a very boggy spot where she sank down nearly to her belly. She led me to a blackened heap of straw left from last year's stacks. Here she flushed a double and a common snipe. I had time only to get the double snipe, but she found the other and I bagged it too, and so it went on and on.

The marshes extended for five versts and the sun was setting fast. I was so excited I prayed to it to stay up a little longer, but it went mercilessly down, and darkness began to fall. By now I was shooting at random without seeing my sights properly.

When I came out of the marshes into the stubble I winced with pain: the stubble was lacerating my blistered feet badly, and as for my sandals I had never noticed losing them in the bog somewhere.

After many long and successful shoots in the Lyakhova marshes I happened to come to the boggy clearing where Kate had once play-acted at the risk of her life. The memory some dogs have is amazing: once more she started for precisely the same old empty spot, but the scent of a live snipe got the better of her passion for acting and, forgetting her airs and graces, she led me to the bird. I failed to take aim when the snipe was rising and swung the barrel of my gun following its flight until there was a sort of imaginary funnel, and sighting for the center of it, I fired and saw the bird fall in the thicket. This time I decided to try Kate at retrieving and back she came with the snipe in her mouth.

Yarik's Love

Sometimes when I take a dog out into the woods I try to use no human language but explain everything by facial expression, gestures, or at most by inarticulate sounds. This is far from easy but this silent communion with your dog does sharpen your faculties and helps you to understand the animal's mind. That is why I think I understood the love of Yarik and Kate better in their silence than if they had been able to talk to one another and I could have overheard them.

Their meeting was none too friendly. He sniffed at her, she did not like it, he walked off and lay down in his corner sulking. But from this moment his character changed: from the age of six weeks our ginger pet had been used to our undivided affection. I am not trying to pretend that animals are more human or perfect than they really are but I can prove that a gun-dog of a good breed is linked with its master through their game tracking by a stronger instinct even than hunger: no matter how hungry Yarik might be, he would always leave his food the moment he saw me with a gun. Nor could this bond be destroyed even by love at the point of its culmination.

It happened soon after Kate came. She gave the first sign of being in heat and we had to put Yarik in the barn with the hound Solovei. Ignoring her condition, I kept training her in the woods and marshes, for we lived a long way from any village and there was little danger of meeting other dogs. Reflecting on the strength of the hunting instinct in dogs one day I decided to risk taking Kate and Yarik out together. That was dangerous not only because the German pointer might copulate with the Irish setter somewhere in the bushes and present me with perfectly useless mongrels, but also because Kate would have to miss another year of training which would probably spoil her for good. Yet spurred by my curiosity about the canine mind, I decided to risk it and sent them both first into the field and then the bushes. I had a few very anxious moments that day when both dogs vanished into the thicket and failed to return. I dashed after them, could not find them and ran the whole circle. No sign of them and no response to my whistling. I lost my head completely and rushed aimlessly into the underbrush cursing myself for my risky venture. At last I spotted Kate in her brown and white coat, and keeping her in sight I ran my anxious eyes about and found Yarik, close by her. With a stare fixed frenziedly on an invisible bird in the grass, he stood like a graven image; a little behind him stood Kate, still innocent of the passion of the chase and visibly perplexed, shedding drops of crimson blood on the grass and forest flowers. And yet they could have used the time they had quite differently. So I had been right after all. That is why they are called gun-dogs: the art from which they gain nothing for themselves is dearer to them than the very passion that keeps the whole world turning.

I came home quite happy. This experiment gives me the courage to confess that I, too, had once missed my chance and let my Kate go, driven by passion for some invisible goal. I was glad to learn that this could happen not only to people, but also to an animal of the highest breed.

I had to keep Yarik in the barn a few days longer in company with Solovei, but I often visited and petted him, calling him a special name I invented for him, and when I petted Kate I called her differently

too. This is my own idea—a double name for my dogs: one for use
at work and the other at home, one for blind obedience, the other
for letting the dog occasionally act the despot. Just try and stick to
the role of a strict trainer when Yarik with his forepaws crossed is
lying sphinx-like on the window-sill, with the sun shining on his coat
in those tones to which Titian alone could do justice. In moments
like these I would say to him, "Kiryusha, my sweet."

He would not stir, knowing full well that I was just admiring him,
and even stiffening in his proud pose.

But if I called, "Yarik," be it very softly, he would do something
with his ears, beam happily, disturb the beauty of his pose, and tapping, sweep the floor with his long-haired tail.

Though I had a man-to-man talk with Yarik in the barn after the
incident in the forest, I sensed a certain estrangement in his proud
manner. When Kate's first heat was over and we brought him back
to the house, his manner was entirely different too. The sound of
soup being poured into the dogs' bowl, brought Kate to the scene,
wagging her stumpy tail eagerly. In the old days Yarik, too, came
hurrying to the sound, but now he ignored it completely as he lay in
his corner: he had his pride and knew where he wasn't wanted. He
carried things so far that even when actually called to eat he got up
with a great show of reluctance. Instead of watching us eat our dinner
in hopes of titbits he calmly sprawled under the table. Kate, on the
other hand, gazed at us with such avid expectation that it made us
sick and we drove her away. But even then Yarik remained stubbornly
indifferent. And we all understood that this was a changed Yarik and
that he would ever hold Kate's coming against us.

When the season began I, failing to appreciate Kate's abilities, did
all my shooting with Yarik. Once again he took up his old position
in the household, was the first to reach the bowl, and watched us at
dinner, while Kate waggled her stump and looked at us in such an
unpleasantly eloquent way that she often got the order: "To your
place!" But towards the end of the season Kate proved so superior
that Yarik seemed dull in comparison. I was fascinated by the quiet
clever work of the German pointer. I decided to switch to the breed
altogether and wanted some puppies from her. The only eligible mate
for her in the neighbourhood was Jack, who belonged to an artist I
knew. We decided to try the two dogs together during the double
snipe migrating flight. They were splendid. Lost in admiration of
their artistic work, we often forgot to take aim. They would go their

separate ways, come together, halt in their tracks, then lead on, and make the final point, glancing back at us anxiously if we tarried. After the shoot we boiled a kettle over a fire and talked about the future offspring of our German Continental, while the dogs, dead tired, lay asleep at our feet. They could sleep in peace with no anxiety about God's vagaries: we were their gods and their fate lay in our hands.

One day the boys and I were left to ourselves in the house. Kate began frolicking with Yarik, and we allowed them to romp round the table, overturn the chairs, jump on the sofa and even pull down the tablecloth, tea things and all. We did not even restrain them when, hot and tired, they began to lap our drinking water. We were infected by their madness and wanted to see it out. At first Yarik, his senses stirred, threw himself on the floor and sprawled belly upwards. Kate pounced on him, harassing and teasing him until he lay helpless and gasping with his tongue lolling. Agile and lithe as a snake, inexhaustible in new tricks, Kate finally got him excited to a pitch. He jumped up suddenly, caught her neck hard with his paws and tried to cover her. She stopped for a moment as though reflecting, then bared her teeth in a snarl, turned and bit him hard. With his tail between his legs, all ruffled and pitiful, he slunk back to his mat and lay there for a long time, a fixed stare in his human dark-circled eyes.

He did not respond to her advances on the next day and just snarled when she got too playful. Undaunted, she leapt over him, nibbling at his ears and tail, and worrying him until tufts of his ginger hair came flying. Now, Yarik had a trick of catching us out whenever we tied a titbit to a piece of string and waved it over his nose. He would pretend to pay no attention, watching and calculating all the while, and then suddenly snap in the air, never missing. So in his game with Kate, he bided his time, measuring the distance and then made an accurate leap, forgetting only one thing—he had no chance whatever for the time of her second heat had not yet come. And all he got for his pains was a fierce bite—the deepest humiliation for an animal as proud as Yarik. He made another try, ignoring the first warning, got another nip and tried again, but was eventually forced back into his corner. He must have seen himself as he really was then: just a wretched cur, bitten and humiliated. He kept licking his wounds all day and paced the room all night. I woke up and opened the door thinking that he wanted to go out. But when he came back he went on with his pacing, back and forth. Through my broken sleep I could hear his claws tapping on the floor all night.

In the morning I noticed signs of Kate's second heat, jotted down the date, and banished Yarik to the barn to stay with Solovei. The rest happened according to the manual on breeding dogs. On the eleventh day Boris Ivanovich turned up with Jack. We put him in with Kate and their love was consummated in exactly fifteen minutes.

The mornings and evenings were frosty. Snow fell at night but the wind blew the snowy powder off our hill and it stood gleaming in dazzling silver. New, summery clouds piled high above the snows, scraps of blue sky showed through the trees, the crows clamoured furiously, and the tomtits sang their mating songs, while the vixens shed blood on their tracks.

The sixty-three-day canine pregnancy was coming to a close. Even Kate's tiny front nipples had swelled, and the two rows stood out in even ridges, making one think of the ones which had miraculously suckled Romulus and Remus. Kate was not ugly even in the last days, for her burden was below, close to the ground, and there it was appropriate and fine. We bought a lot of beef bones, made an excellent broth, and adding oatmeal to it gave her as much as she could eat. But she always left something in her bowl and Yarik would emerge from under the bench, come up cautiously and eat what was left: he was altogether humbled and subdued. All day long he would lie on the window-sill in his leonine pose, his paws crossed, basking in the sun and probably dreaming of the coming spring and the migrating birds. I too spent a lot of my time gazing out of the window and we would very often turn our heads in the same direction, watching something in the snow outside. I was working out a new plan of training in which no words would be used and all orders would be given with eyes or gestures alone. If I could do this, I would come closer to a complete understanding of a dog's mind, and then perhaps of their love so that I should be able to explain Yarik's feelings during Kate's pregnancy.

While I sat there thinking about this and all sorts of other things, turning my head with Yarik's to follow the blue shadows of the roving clouds, Kate had been looking for me. She saw me by the window, ran up and lay down at my feet. She seemed to be asking for something. I got up and she ran for the door. I went out with her. She relieved herself quickly and hurried back. I did not understand the urgency of the moment and stayed for a while alone in the yard. The moment I walked back into the house I heard a peculiar sound coming from Kate's room: she was licking and lapping at something. I went in and saw a blind little pup at her side with exactly the same coffee-coloured spots as her own. There was no need to help her because she did everything herself with teeth and tongue, nipping, swallowing, and cleaning so nicely that the white of the puppies' coats gleamed like the virgin snow. It was all going well until after she had her fifth, and then the whites of her eyes turned blue, she weakened and collapsed. We gave her some wine and she was delivered of the sixth and last, the eagerly awaited Remus. We wanted males particularly and there had been only one before: Romulus.

After a few minutes of self-midwifery and cleaning up, there was not a spot anywhere and the well-groomed blind puppies were crawling one over another with squeals until they finally found what they needed and began to suckle. And now those who love life should look into the mother's eyes, but silently, for words would be sacrilegious. . . .

And so we stood and looked when suddenly there was a sharp change. The mother began to tremble, her eyes flashed evilly, her hair bristled from neck to tail. We looked round and saw Yarik's ginger head at the door. He had come to have a look too. Fortunately for him he managed to swerve just in time and she sank her teeth into his hind leg and not his throat. He was off with a squeal, pursued right to the kitchen. She came back and lay trembling all over till evening.

We had guests that day and I told them the story of the dogs' love, of the way Yarik had stood pointing at invisible game ignoring Kate in her first heat, of the way they had romped about for a whole month that winter, of Jack, and of Kate's inexplicable rage when Yarik had poked his head into the room wanting to have a peep too.

"Why inexplicable?" said a lady, well versed in matters of love. "If I had a lover like Yarik I would have torn him to bits."

"But it wasn't his fault," I said. "It was we, their gods, who changed the course of their romance, replacing Yarik with Jack."

"But gods are not infallible," retorted the lady. "He had his chance in the bushes, and instead he stood there pointing at what he could not see, the fool."

The Marshes

I know there are few people who have ever spent hours of waiting in the marshes to hear the mating call of the black grouse in early spring, yet I lack words to give even a pale description of all the magnificence of this marshland concert in the hour before sunrise. I have often noticed that the curlew was the one to sound the first note long before there was any hint of light in the sky. He trills a very thin note, quite unlike his usual whistling. Later, when the willow-ptarmigan begin to call, the grouse-hens to cluck and the blackcock to mutter right close to your tent, you can't be bothered with the curlew any longer, but when the sun comes out in all its splendor you are sure to notice his new tune, a very jolly one, like a folk dance. This dance tune is no less essential in welcoming the sun in than the crane's call. One morning I looked out of my tent and saw a grey curlew, a female, sitting on a hummock amid a throng of blackcocks. A male curlew flew down to her, he flapped his large wings to keep afloat, hardly touching her back with his feet, and sang his folk dance tune. And then all the birds of the marshes joined in song, the very air quivered with sound, and I remember a puddle rippling on a perfectly windless day with the world of insects aroused in it.

The sight of a curlew's long, hooked beak invariably takes my fancy back to the days before the first man appeared in the world. But then everything about the marshes is weird, they are so little known, neither written about nor painted, that when you are there you do feel as though man has not yet been created.

I took my dogs out for a run in the marshes one evening. Rain was just over and it was stuffy before the next cloud-burst. The dogs ran about with tongues lolling, they flopped into puddles now and then and lay wallowing there like pigs. Evidently the young birds had not hatched yet and our marshlands, so crammed with game, had no scent to offer the dogs, and so even a passing crow got them all excited. Suddenly a large bird appeared and with shrill cries began to describe huge circles over our heads. Another curlew joined the first and, crying, wheeled overhead, then a third one—evidently from a different flock—flew across the path of the circling two and disappeared. I had to get a curlew's egg for my collection; I reckoned they would narrow their circles as I neared the nest and widen them as I receded from it, and so I began my game of blind man's buff, guided by the sound of their cries. Moving about slowly I finally sensed the nearness of the nest when the sun was already a low-hanging great ball, glowing crimson in the warm and plentiful vapours. The birds were crying stridently and wheeling so close to me that against the crimson skies I could clearly see their long hooked beaks, gaping to let out their incessant panicky cry. And now my dogs, catching the scent in the air, made a point. I followed the direction of their eyes and noses and saw two large eggs, with no sort of nest or protection for them, lying on a dry yellow strip of moss beside a tiny shrub. Ordering the dogs to lie still, I looked about me happily, heedless of the angry sting of mosquitoes attacking me in swarms. It was good to be in these inaccessible marshes and to get the feel of the world long, long ago breathed by these curved-winged birds with their long hooked beaks silhouetted against the red disc of the sun.

I made to stoop down and pick up one of those large beautiful eggs, when suddenly I saw a man walking straight towards me across the marsh. He had neither gun, dog, nor even a stick; no one could have come here in passing and I knew of no one who like myself would find pleasure in rambling over this swamp pestered by swarms of mosquitoes. I resented him as much as I would an unkind stranger who had caught me making faces into a looking-glass. I actually walked away from the spot and did not take the egg, knowing that the stranger's inquisitive questions would ruin this moment of bliss for me. I called my dogs and led them up a rise. I sat down on a stone so thickly covered with yellow lichen that it made quite a warm seat. The moment I had walked away from the nest the birds widened their circles, but I could no longer enjoy watching them. The stranger coming towards me put me on edge. I could make him out clearly now: he was middle-aged, very lean, he walked slowly, his attention on the circling birds. I drew an easier breath when I saw him change his direction, go up another rise, sit on a stone and freeze to immobility. I rather liked to feel there was another human being there, contemplating the evening with reverence. It seemed we understood one another without a word, for words would be superfluous. And now I watched with redoubled interest the birds crossing the red disc of the sun; my thoughts were curiously divided between the great age of the world and the brevity of the history of mankind; how short it was really.

The sun went down. I looked round to see my friend but he was gone. The birds calmed their cries and must have gone to their nests. Telling my dogs to follow me quietly I made for the nest on noiseless feet, wondering if I could catch a glimpse of those birds close to. I easily found the spot by the tiny shrub and it amazed me how near the birds were letting me come. At last I crept up to the shrub and paused in astonishment: there was nothing there. I touched the moss: it still felt warm where the warm eggs had been lying.

All I had done was look at the eggs, but the birds fearing a man's evil eye, had lost no time in hiding them away.

The Warmer Place

Whenever Nerle came back from our shoots in the marshes cold and dripping, her mother Kenta warned her with a yap, knowing very well that Nerle would try to snuggle up to her to get warm. But when it was Kenta who came back, Nerle—young and inquisitive—would leap up from her mat at once, eager to know what we had brought, and then Kenta would lie down in her warm place. When I had no intention of going out and just dropped in to see how the dogs were, they would both jump up, pleading:

"Take me, take me."

I would stroke both of them in turn and each would think that she would go and not the other.

In their excitement they would put their paws on my chest. But this was strictly forbidden and I would give the order, "No shooting today. Down Nerle, down Kenta!"

And back they would go to their mats, but Kenta invariably chose Nerle's place, and Nerle her mother's, each certain that the other's was a warmer place than her own.

The Riddles of the Woods

There were plenty of black grouse in the forest: all the ant-hills were scratched by their claws. But one ant-hill had a peculiar look, there was a deep hole bored in it. No black grouse could have made it, and I could not imagine what woodland creature had broken so cruelly into the ants' republic.

It was rather annoying to be unable to solve a woodland riddle, but nature posed thousands of them and one could find an answer for them nowhere except in one's own head. Usually I left the problem unanswered, but kept it in mind trusting that some day I should find the solution in the same woods.

I remember that as a young man I wondered a lot about the origin of the grassy hummocks in the marshes. I read up on the subject, but none of the answers were really satisfactory. They were numerous enough, but all of them were somehow vague and conjectural. On one of my rambles I sat down to rest in a woodland clearing. There were many tree-stumps in this damp spot, and between them a fresh carpet of moss. It was of a most beautiful green colour, almost as though the moon, rather than the sun, were shining on it. And the moonlit green carpet was spread over tiny bumps. That was how the hummocks started, I thought. Though it was plain enough how the hummocks would grow, it was not at all clear how they had come into being in the first place. I used my hands then, pulling away the mossy covering and exposing a rotting birch-stump underneath. So that was what caused hummocks.

I have noticed that problems crop up mostly when I'm walking and the answers come when I sit down to rest. The same thing happened with the curiously dented ant-hill. I felt like having a cup of tea, unscrewed the top of my thermos flask, sat down on a soft mossy hillock under a pine-tree and began to sip the tea slowly, musing and gradually merging with the life around me. A warm dark rain-cloud covered the sun and then everything around me seemed to be musing too. In the perfect silence which falls before rain I could hear the distant flutter of a woodpecker growing louder and louder until—hello—there he was perched in the pine-tree right over me. He then pondered something for a while and looked round once or twice, though, curiously enough, he never glanced at me, the terrible monster below. I have often noted this about birds: they cock their heads from side to side but never look down. Not woodpeckers alone but a black grouse too had sometimes sat on a branch just above me while I drank my woodland tea. Taking no notice of me whatever, the woodpecker came down on the very ant-hill that had puzzled me, and there was the solution before my eye: he dived into the hole and busied himself there foraging for food.

And one day that summer—and what a day it was!—so many riddles came up all at once that I was driven into cursing a perfectly innocent old woman. To begin with, Nerle, a young dog then going through her first year of training, got completely out of hand in the marshes. She ignored my whistle and let the snipe fly up without pointing. I lost my temper because I wanted to do some shooting just then and not training. I missed time and again, rushing after the dog, chasing the snipe, too flurried to rid myself of a bee buzzing in my hair. At last I pulled myself together, called the dog back, took off my hat, and ruffled my hair until the buzzing stopped.

I felt better after that and keen to resume my shooting, I unleashed Nerle once more, but when she was about fifty paces away from the bird she started stealing upon it again. I rushed to check her advance, and landed with both feet in a cow's cake. As I got out of it I heard that tiresome bee buzzing in my hair again with all its might.

"Click, click," a snipe again flew up without Nerle's point, and I was too late to take aim. A fine bird it was, too. Suddenly I thought I heard the whirr again but nothing flew up. This was quite remarkable. And again I heard the same sound behind me. I wheeled round, but saw nothing. I listened hard but there was only the bee buzzing in my hair and a magpie chattering in the thicket. I decided that flustered as I was I had mistaken the magpie's chatter for the snipe, when suddenly again there was a "click," which had nothing to do with the magpie. It was at this point that I was driven to cursing that old woman, who, instead of wishing me the customary: "Neither feather nor fur," in the kindness of her heart, wished me: "God help you to get a full bag!"

Utterly worn out I got to a dry patch of land, sat down on some thin logs chopped down by somebody, took my hat off and went through my hair thoroughly. I found no bee, though, and the buzzing had stopped. My strength came back to me slowly and with it my usual confidence that understanding would help me solve any difficulties I had with the dog. I believe understanding is essential because no two individual creatures of nature are exactly alike; man or animal, each differs from its fellows and so it will do no good to go by a fixed rule; a fresh clue has to be found in every case.

Meanwhile, Nerle got up quietly, sniffed at something on the ground, looked at me timidly and began to move in a narrow circle—and then wider and wider. "What did I say?" I said softly to remind her of my order to lie down.

She came nearer but still describing her circles, and half-way to me she started off again. "What did I say?" I repeated.

I noticed that Nerle, ordered to lie still and follow no scent on the ground, was trying hard to hold her nose as high as possible to make up for it. This gave me an idea.

I got up and went forward but as soon as she had run further than ten paces away from me I quietly repeated, "What did I say?" In this way we got to a clump of bushes. She halted in her tracks and I said again, "What did I say?" holding her to her point. Then a black snipe flew out.

Naturally, I hurried back to the marsh keeping her from ranging more than ten paces, and so she kept straining upward to scent the bird. When she did and was making for it, I said, "What did I say?"

She stopped, holding her nose high and sucking in the air. She raised a hind leg first but finding this awkward bent up a front one. Water dripped from it in a little pool.

I shot that snipe, then another, and then a third, removing with my shrewdness and stubbornness the spell of the old woman whom I had cursed for no fault of hers at all. I solved the riddle of the bee as well. It was not buzzing in my hair but behind my hat band. As for the snipe's "click," it turned out to be my own nose: when I breathed too deeply, there was a boggy squelch that was much like a snipe's click.

The Shepherd's Pipe

We've had the same shepherd in Pereslavl country for years but we never heard him pipe, only whistle. But over in Zabolotye the shepherd blows a horn and his boy plays a pipe called *zhaleika* at dawn, and I feel like a sinner who has overslept the morning service if I fail to get up to hear his tune on the pipe made of mezereon with a reed mouthpiece and a cow's horn resonator. At last I was tempted to try my hand at this music of the marshes, and had a *zhaleika* made.

I have a fairly good ear and even managed one of Chaikovsky's songs on my new instrument but I just couldn't produce our shepherd's simple tune, and I gave it up.

One day it had been raining from early morning and I stayed at home writing. Towards evening the rain stopped, but the setting sun was cold and yellow. I went out on to the porch and, facing the sunset, began to play my pipe. Perhaps it was the sunset, or the tree—that large willow by the roadside that in the twilight or at dawn looks very much like a peasant with a big nose and dishevelled hair—I don't know what inspired me, but I looked and looked at this head and suddenly found it all very simple. One should leave the operas and Chaikovsky alone—just finger the holes, and the little pipe will do the rest.

Some village women came over and sat on the bench.

"Well, am I much worse than the shepherd from over the marshes?" I asked.

"You're better," they said.

I played on. The afterglow of the sun died away. A cart loaded with peasants appeared on the road. They would laugh at me. That would finish it, I thought. But to my surprise they stopped the horse and stayed to listen with the women.

I finished playing and slipped quickly into the house. The window was open and I heard a peasant say as he started the horse:

"Must've stuffed himself full."

"Sure, catch him playing on an empty stomach," remarked another.

From which I gathered that the peasants had taken me for the shepherd, who was given shelter and board in each house by turn. They thought he was staying in a well-to-do house and was playing after a good supper.

FALL

The Eyes of the Earth

Nothing but cold, rain and wind from morning till night! I have heard women who have lost their near and dear ones say that sometimes a man's eyes die before his consciousness. Sometimes a dying man will actually say, "I can't see you, my dears." That means his eyes are dead already and the next moment his tongue may fail him. It was like that with the lake at my feet. The lakes are the eyes of the earth in folklore. And here I could bear witness that it was true—the eyes die first, sensitive to the death of the light. The beautiful struggle for light is just beginning in the forest, with the tree-tops bursting into flame—and throwing off a light of their own it seems—but the water lies dead, a cold grave for cold fishes.

The rains had long been plaguing the peasants. The martins had flown away. The swallows were flocking in the fields. We had two frosts already. The lime-trees were yellow from top to bottom and the potato stalks had grown black. Flax was spread for bleaching everywhere. The double snipe had appeared, and the evening shoots began.

The Thief's Cap's on Fire*

The gold of the leaves never stirred and hoary linens were spread over the grass—a real frost, not just cold dew. It wasn't till eight in the morning that this visible frost turned to dew and the linens under the bushes disappeared. The leaves kept fluttering down. In the distance the fir and pine were saying good-bye to the birches while the

---

* A proverb probably originating from the story about a man who cried, "The thief's cap's on fire" to startle and so discover the thief.

tall, fiery-capped aspens towered over the forest, and for some reason
I remembered the old saying which had somewhat puzzled me in my
far-away childhood: The thief's cap's on fire.

But the swallows were still here.

Birds' Sleep

The spiders had grown numb from the cold, and their webs were
rent by the wind and the rain. The sturdiest, though, made with the
spiders' best, remained intact in spite of the weather, capturing anything that could move in the air. But the only flying things now were
the leaves. And so a glowing autumn leaf edged with drops of dew
was caught in a web and rocked by the wind as in an invisible ham-
mock. The sun came out for a moment and the dew-drops sparkled
like diamonds. This caught my eye and reminded me of my intention
to learn something of the wood-grouse in this season when the autumn leaves become their favourite delicacy. I have often heard and
read that wood-grouse fly to the aspens an hour before sunset, and
peck the leaves till dark, roosting in the trees overnight and pecking
a little more in the morning.

I happened upon them in a small clearing deep in the forest. As
I waded across the stream one of my boots squelched in the mud,
scaring a hen-grouse from an aspen directly overhead. This tall tree
stood at the very edge of the forest thick with aspens and birches; it
was the struggle for life against pine and fir that had made them
grow so tall. A forest road, black and rutted, ran close to the trees,
and the falling aspen leaves left a bright yellow trail on the black. It
was very difficult stealing across these pale patches because the wood-
grouse were all up in the aspens now and could easily see me. The
clearing was a new one—last winter's, and the firewood which had
not been carted away then had darkened, no longer visible among
the vigorous growth of young aspen saplings with their large, bright
leaves. On the older aspens, however, the leaves were almost yellow,
and so I crept stealthily from one old tree to the next. There was a
light drizzle and a soft wind, the aspens murmured and rustled,
raindrops rapped and tapped and through all this I could not hear
the birds ripping the leaves. But suddenly a wood-grouse flew up
from one of the saplings and settled on a tree about two hundred
paces from me on the other side of the clearing. I stood watching
the bird nibbling at the leaves and gulping them down. When sudden

stillness followed a gust of wind, I could hear the leaves being ripped quite distinctly. I had heard the sound before. When the bird had nibbled all the tastier leaves from the branch, it hopped down to a lower one, but this was too thin to support it and so it slid on down steadying itself with its wings. Soon I heard the same fluttering and crackling on my side of the clearing and realized that there were feeding birds hidden in the aspens all around. In the daytime they must have wandered about the clearing, catching insects or swallowing those tiny stones so necessary to them, while at night they went up into the branches to enjoy their favourite delicacy before going to sleep.

The west wind slackened by sundown as is usual in our part of the world. The sun suddenly flooded the forest with all its rays. I cupped my hand behind my ear and I could just distinguish the ripping of the leaves above—a muffled and yet sharper sound than the hollow dripping of water. Then I got up and moved in on it stealthily. This was not like hopping upon a bird in spring, when it's deaf to everything but its own song hurled into the blue. I found it hardest to cross a large pool, for though strewn with a thick carpet of aspen leaves, it was very muddy and deep. I had to arch my instep like a ballet dancer every time I drew my foot out so the mud would not squelch. And whenever a drop of water fell into the pool from my carefully raised foot, it sounded terribly loud. Yet a mouse scurried across under the leaves cutting a furrow through and making so much noise that I'm sure if it had been my doing the birds would have flown long ago. The sound must have been familiar to the birds, who knew it was just a mouse running past. And if a fox snapped a twig, the bird would probably know it was a fox that meant it no harm going about its business. For in woodland, all things have their meaning and associations. But there is no telling what a man might be up to, and therefore the sounds he makes clash so violently with the rest.

A passion for a thing, however, begets unbelievable patience, and given the time I might have attained cat-like agility, but time was almost up, the sun went down, and soon it would be too dark to shoot. I had no doubt that my bird was in the aspen in front of me, in the branches behind. But I neither ventured nor had the time to get to the other side of it. What was to be done then? There was one tiny opening in the aspen's yellow crown giving a glimpse of the sky—a little skylight that kept opening and closing. I knew it was the bird pecking at the leaves, its head blocking out the skylight, and I could even make out its tiny beard. Few men could shoot on the spur of the moment as well as I, but just then an invisible twig snapped under my foot, and the skylight stood open. . . . What was even worse—the bird, sensing danger, began to snort as though cursing me. Another disappointment—a bird on a nearby branch slid down and for a moment was revealed to me completely. I could neither hit it from that distance nor make a move to come closer for it would have certainly spotted me. I froze to a standstill on one foot while the other, which had snapped the twig, was almost unsupported. Other birds came to settle for the night all around. One of them began to cluck in the tall aspen, dropping little twigs, cut away obliquely, by which we can always tell the night perches of the grouse. The first bird was gradually reassured: it must have been sitting there with its neck craned and head cocked. Down below where I stood and the mouse still rustled, it grew quite dark. The second bird had vanished in the gloom. Probably all the others had gone to sleep with their bearded heads under their wings. I shifted my foot which had gone to sleep and with relief leaned back against the same tree in which the bird I had disturbed must have now been peacefully asleep.

One lacks words to describe what the deep forest is like at night when you know that the great birds are asleep overhead, the last survivors of an age of great creatures. They are restless sleepers too: one will toss, another preen itself or click its bill. I was not afraid to be alone, rather the contrary, I felt as if I were visiting my family on a holiday. If not for the cold and damp, I might have gone to sleep right there with them. There must have been a pool nearby for I heard the drops falling upon it from the tall trees, from high branches and lower ones, big drops and small ones. When I took in these sounds and understood them, they merged into a harmony that was more beautiful than the ordinary good music I used to enjoy. And when everything nocturnal had found its place in the melody of raindrops, I suddenly heard a most incongruous sound—snoring.

It was not fear, but the intrusion of this incongruous sound into my marvellous concert that made me hurry away from a virgin forest where someone was snoring so disgustingly.

As I walked through the village on my way home it seemed to me, after that snoring in the forest, that everything and everyone was snoring, both beast and man. And when I came to the house, Seryozha, our landlady's son, was snoring ferociously in the pantry while Domna Ivanovna herself and the rest of the family snored away in the kitchen. But strangest of all, besides the snoring of the cattle in the yard, I heard the finer snores of some other creatures, and using my torchlight I discovered that this came from the geese and fowls.

And even in my sleep this snoring haunted me. I recalled, as one sometimes does in dreams, things that could never come back again. All my old bird dreams crowded my sleep that night. . . .

And suddenly I realized that it was the wood-grouse who snored in the woods and no other. I jumped out of bed, drank some cold tea, took my gun and hurried to my old place in the woods. I stood leaning back against the same tree and waited for sunrise. Now, after hearing the snores of fowl and beast I could identify the snoring not only of the bird roosting overhead but also of the one in the next tree.

The snoring ceased when the herald of the dawn piped and the woods grew lighter. The skylight in my aspen was open again but the head did not appear. It was a cloudless morning and the light was coming on fast. The bird in the next tree stirred, thus revealing itself: I could see it perfectly well. Fully awake now, it stuck out its head like a fist on its long neck, now to one side now to the other, and suddenly spread its tail as in the mating season. I had heard about autumn mating songs and wondered if it would call. But instead it pulled in its tail and began pecking at the leaves with amazing speed. My own bird must have begun nibbling at the leaves just then, for I saw its head popping over the little skylight.

My shot was so accurate that it hardly stirred when it dropped but merely clawed at the bark of the aspen. And the leaves it let loose were still floating down.

Coming back to those snores, I suppose that the sound comes from the fluttering feathers when a large bird breathes under its wing in sleep. However, I shouldn't swear to it that wood-grouse do sleep with their heads under their wings. I am judging by the domestic fowl. It's all surmises, stories and speculation, whereas the real world of the woods is little known.

The Dead Lake

It was quiet in the golden woods and as warm as in summer. Gossamer settled in the fields, the dry leaves rustled crisply underfoot, the birds flushed up well out of range, and I saw a hare throw up a cloud of dust in the road. I left the house early with a headache, and walked and walked until I was too tired to think. All I could do was follow the dog, hold the gun at the ready, and glance at my compass from time to time. I wandered on and on until I saw by my compass that I was far on my way in the opposite direction to home. I had never been in this part of the country before. I struggled through the thick underbrush and suddenly I came upon a large, perfectly round dead lake framed in thickly wooded golden-leafed shores. I sat there for a long time, gazing into these dead eyes of the earth.

There was a sudden change of weather in the evening, a huge samovar seemed to have come to a boil somewhere beyond the forest. This was the rain and wind unclothing the trees. That night, according to all signs and my notes, the geese were to fly away.

Flurry of First Snow

The moonlit night was still, with a light frost, and a flurry of snow came with daybreak. The squirrels were chasing one another over the bare branches. I thought I heard a black grouse crowing, and I had half a mind to go for him when I realized that this was not the cry of a bird but the clatter of a cart on a distant road.

It was a patchy sort of day with spells of sunshine and clouds of scurrying snow. At nine in the morning there was still a film of ice on the marshes and white cloths were spread over the tree-stumps upon which lay the aspen leaves like blood-red saucers. A small snipe flew from the swamp and disappeared into the snowy distance.

The geese were flocking. As I stood still in the twilight watching the sunset I heard the cries of flying geese, and a flock of teals flew over and then another of some large ducks. I grew so excited whenever I saw a new flock that I lost the thread of my thoughts and could pick it up again only with some difficulty. What I was thinking about was: how wonderfully it was all arranged that each of us had not too long to live and therefore could not taste everything there was, and so the world to us appeared infinite in its variety.

Geese and Swans

It had been a clear, very cold night, bright with moonlight and stars. Everything was white that morning. The geese were busy feeding. A new flock joined them and some two hundred were now flying from the lake to the fields. Till midday the black grouse kept in the trees, muttering away. Then the sky clouded, and it turned cold and raw.

The sun appeared again in the afternoon and the weather kept fine until evening. To our joy our two golden birches had survived the general holocaust. The wind came from the north, however, and the lake was black and wrathful. A great flock of swans had come. I heard that swans usually stayed with us for a long time; when the lake froze over and only a narrow pool remained in the middle and carts were driven straight across the ice, one could sometimes hear a low chatter through the gloom, as though people were talking, but it was only the swans in the ice-free pool.

I crept up to the geese in the evening and could have wrought havoc among them, but after climbing the steep bank I was badly out of breath or perhaps I was just not in the mood. There was a stump at the edge of a gully and I sat down for a rest. I only had to lift my head and there was the ryefield with the geese—some ten paces away. I had my gun ready and even if they had taken fright suddenly they could not have got away without losses. I lit a cigarette, waving the smoke from my lips with my hand. There was another gully beyond and a fox stole out of it, taking advantage of the dusk just as I had done. Before I could raise my gun the whole flock swished up and was out of range. A good thing I had guessed it was a fox, and did not lift my head at once. He was following the tracks of the birds like a dog and came closer and closer. I steadied my elbows, took aim and whistled softly like a mouse. He looked my way, and I whistled again—the fox came towards me.

The Shadow of Man

There was a morning moon. The eastern sky was clouded. At long last a strip of dawn showed from under the heavy blanket, and the moon floated in deeper blue.

The lake seemed to be covered with floes, so queerly and abruptly had the mist broken up. The village cocks and swans gave voice.

I am not much of a musician, but I think that the swan's highest note is the same as the crane's when it summons day to break in the marshes. And its lowest note is like that of the geese, when they gabble and grumble in basso.

I cannot say whether it was the faint blue light of the moon or the morning glow in the blue around it that made me notice the rooks. Soon I could see that rooks and jackdaws were virtually swarming in the sky: the rooks were manoeuvring before migration and the jackdaws, as usual, were seeing them off. Who could tell me why the jackdaws always came to see the rooks off? There was a time when I thought that everything was known and that only I, poor wretch, knew nothing. But later I discovered that learned men may not know the simplest things about living nature.

After this, I began to puzzle things out for myself. In this matter of jackdaws it seems to me that the bird's mind is much like a wave: some impulse is transmitted from generation to generation like a wave spread by a stone thrown into the water. At the dawn of the impulse the daws and rooks must have gathered to fly away together. But the rooks had flown away while the daws changed their mind for some reason or other and stayed behind. And they repeated this from generation to generation ever since. They gather to fly away together, but then the daws return after seeing the rooks off.

But perhaps it was even simpler than that. We have learned only recently that some of our common crows migrate. Why then could not some of our jackdaws fly off with the rooks?

A fresh wind rose in the morning and felled the small fir-tree I had planted in the middle of the field in order to steal up on the geese. I went over to set it up again when the geese suddenly appeared. I took cover behind my tree but saw them circle over it, clearly suspicious, and finally fly off and settle near Dubovitsi. I tried to stalk them from behind a large willow bush in the middle of a clearing. The stubble was covered with hoar-frost and my shadow crept over the white a long way ahead of me. I did not notice it at first, but then I realized with dismay that my shadow, enormous and terrifying, was stealing upon the flock. The shadow wavered, there was a terrific commotion, and the whole flock rose up with a shout two hundred voices strong, each as loud as a soldier's hurrah in an attack, and made for my bush. I barely managed to jump into the clump and thrust my two barrels out to meet the long-necked assault.

Squirrels

At the first streak of light we went to the fir coppice after squirrels, going singly and taking different paths. The sky was heavy and so low that it seemed to be resting on the fir tops, many of which were red with cones; and where there are plenty of cones there are sure to be plenty of squirrels.

Some of the firs look as if a comb had been run through them from top to bottom, others were very fluffy, some were young and full of sap and others old, with grey-green beards of lichens. One very old tree was almost dead at the roots and had a grey-green beard on almost every branch, though there were enough cones in the top to fill a barn. One of the branches quivered, but the squirrel had caught sight of me and grew still. The old tree under which I stood had been singed from below and rose from a dishlike hollow. I raked away the dead leaves that had fallen into the dish from the birches nearby and found the earth to be black underneath and covered with ashes. Now I understood how this dish had come about. Last winter a hunter had stalked a marten here. The animal must have been jumping about from tree to tree, shedding bits of bark and leaving its tracks on the snow-laden branches. The chase after the valuable animal brought the hunter deeper into the woods until darkness fell and he had to spend the night where he was. Under the tree where I stood there had been an enormous ant-hill, possibly the largest ant community in the woods. The hunter had cleared the snow away, set fire to it, and burnt the whole kingdom down. He had made himself comfortable in the warm hollow, covered himself with his coat and slept on the hot ashes, to continue his chase in the morning. In the spring the hollow had filled with water, and in the autumn with the leaves of the birches and the chips of the fir cones shed by the squirrels. And here I was after the squirrel.

I wanted to use the time of waiting for the squirrel to put down some notes about the ant-hill. Very cautiously I took my notebook and pencil from my pocket and wrote that the ant-hill had probably been as great a kingdom of its kind as China is among our human countries. But just as I got to the word China, the chip of a fir cone fell on the page. A squirrel must have been perched right over my head. It had been quiet when I arrived but consumed with curiosity, it wanted to find out whether I was still alive or had turned into a harmless tree-trunk. Perhaps it had dropped that chip on purpose. Then it waited a little and dropped another. Curiosity would not let it move until it had found out. I went on writing about the great kingdom of ants, created with great pains and perseverance; about the giant who had come along and destroyed the kingdom merely to spend a single night in warmth. The squirrel now dropped a whole cone, nearly knocking the notebook out of my hand. Out of the corner of my eye I watched the foolish little thing stealing cautiously down twig by twig until it was looking straight over my shoulder at my lines about the giant destroying the ants' kingdom for one night's sleep.

Another time I shot a squirrel and saw three cones fall from three different firs. A squirrel must have been sitting in each, and startled by the shot gave itself away by dropping a cone.

That is how we hunt squirrels in our Moscow taiga: in November, from dawn until eleven in the morning and from two o'clock until the evening, for it is then that the squirrels peel the cones, sway the branches, nibble at the bark and leap from tree to tree after the choicest cones. We never hunt from eleven to two because that is the time when the squirrels hide in the bushiest branches and wash themselves with their tiny paws.

The Badger

The ground was all white this time last year but now the autumn had overstayed its leave and the white hares could be seen a long way off as they ran or lay down on the black earth: things were hard for them now! But the grey badgers had nothing to be afraid of. They were still about, I thought. How fat they must have grown! I decided to watch for one by its hole. In the pine woods at this gloomy time it is not easy to attain to that peace in which no indoor estimates of dull or fine weather really matter but in which everything moves on, finding its own meaning and joy in this perpetual movement.

The cliff where the badgers lived was so steep in places that one often had to leave his hand's tracks next to those of the badger. I sat down by an old fir-tree to watch the main burrow through a lower branch. A squirrel, lining its winter quarters with moss, dropped a few bits of bark, and then silence fell, the silence that the hunter, sitting by the badger's burrow, can listen to for hours without getting bored.

Under this heavy sky, propped up by the tops of a dense fir forest, there is nothing to hint at the position of the sun, yet the badger in his dark hole knows when the sun sets and a little later cautiously comes out for his nocturnal hunt. He will poke out his nose again and again, sniffing and vanishing, and all at once he will dash out with amazing alacrity, outwitting the watcher. It is better to lie in wait for him before dawn, for on his way back he plays no tricks and his rustling can be heard far away. But at this time of the year he was hibernating, he would not come out every day and it would be a pity to waste a night watching for him and then a day sleeping it off.

It was not like sitting in an arm-chair, of course, and my legs grew numb, but suddenly the badger poked his nose out and at once I felt far more comfortable than in the softest of chairs. He poked out his nose and dived back. Half an hour later he showed up again for a moment, thought a little and vanished for good.

He did not come out at all. I had barely reached the woodman's cottage on my way home when it began to snow. Could the badger have sensed this when he put his nose out?

Wet snow, falling in a straight line, kept settling on the branches, sliding, falling and swishing all night long. The swishing drove the white hare out of the woods; he shrewdly guessed that the black fields would be white by morning and he would be able to lie there undisturbed. And so he chose a spot near the woods and beside him lay a sun-blanched wind-blown skull of a horse, which looked very much like another white hare. By dawn the field was a spotless sheet and both white hare and white skull were swallowed in the white vastness.

We were a bit late; the scent was already fading when we unleashed Osman. When he first sniffed over the terrain he could still distinguish the track of the brown hare from the white one's. He was after the brown. But Osman had barely caught on to the track when the snow melted, leaving neither scent nor prints on the black underneath. We gave it up then and turned for home, walking along the edge of the woods.

"Look through your binoculars," I said to my companion. "What's that over there? That white spot?"

"The skull of a horse," he said.

I took the glasses and looked.

"There is another white spot," he said. "To the left of it."

I looked again and saw the hare, gleaming white like the skull, and I could even see its black eyes against the white. He was in desperate straits. If he stayed where he was anyone could see him, and if he ran he would leave tracks in the wet ground for the dogs to follow. We made up his mind for him. We started him up and off dashed Osman baying furiously.

The Power of Beauty

In the mist the artist Boris Ivanovich stole up very close to the swans and took aim. Thinking, however, that small shot would be better he replaced the cartridge with duck-shot. He took aim again but suddenly he had the disturbing feeling that he was not aiming at swans at all but at human beings. He lowered his gun and feasted his eyes on them, then backed away very cautiously—so cautiously that the swans never knew they had been in mortal danger.

I have heard that the swan is supposed to be an ill-natured bird and cannot tolerate geese or ducks near it, often killing them. Can this be true? Well, even if it is, we shan't let it mar our poetic legend of a young girl transformed into a swan: for such is the power of beauty.

Mist

The night was starry and wonderfully warm. Just before daybreak I went out of doors and heard a solitary drop fall from the roof. The mists uncurled at daybreak and we found ourselves on the shore of a boundless sea.

The most exquisite and mysterious time of the day is that between the first streak of light and sunrise, when the pattern of the leafless trees just begins to be outlined. The birches seem to have been combed downwards, the maples and aspens upwards. I witnessed the birth of the hoar-frost, saw it shrivel and whiten the old yellow grass and glass the puddles with the thinnest film of ice.

When the sun came up the silhouette of the opposite bank emerged from the clouds and hung high in the air. Then the lake came out in the rays of the sun. Everything was magnified in the sunshot mist: the long line of ducks was like an attacking army and the flock of swans like the fairy-tale white marble town rearing in the sea.

A black grouse flew past from the roost—on some important business, obviously, because another was flying in the same direction, and then more and more of them appeared. When I reached the spot near the lake marshes, a large flock had already gathered. A few were perched in the trees but most of them were scampering between the mounds, hopping and cooing as if it were spring.

Only the bright green of the winter rye made the day differ from one in early spring—and perhaps, too, something in oneself: the wine of spring was no longer running in one's veins and joy had lost its poignancy. Joy was serene now like a release from pain. You are glad the pain is over but then you think nostalgically: why, that wasn't just pain, that was life itself that passed.

During this first long spell of frost the lake was utterly black ringed with ice, and with every day the ring of white icy shores was drawn tighter and tighter around the narrowing circle of black water. And now the ring fell apart, the released water sparkled and rejoiced. Streams rushed down the hillsides, gurgling as in spring. But when clouds hid the sun we knew we would have seen neither the water, nor the ducks, nor the white swans but for its rays. Everything was swathed in mist once more, the lake itself was no more and all that remained was the outline of the opposite shore hanging high in the air.

Ivan-and-Marya*—Wild Pansies

Late autumn is just like early spring: a patchwork of white snow and black earth. But in spring it smelled of earth and in autumn of snow. It's always so. We get used to the snow in winter and are sensitive to the smell of earth in spring, but towards autumn this scent grows so habitual that snow smells the stronger.

The sun peeps out rarely now and even then for not more than an hour, but what a joy it is. We thrill at the sight of a few frozen leaves still clinging to a willow-tree in spite of the winds, or a tiny blue flower at our feet.

I stoop for a closer look at this flower and to my amazement it's Ivan: all that is left of the violet and yellow double flower Ivan-and-Marya. Ivan, by the way, is not a flower at all, it's made up of tiny curled leaves and we only call it a flower, because of its violet colour. The yellow Marya is the real flower, pistil and stamens and all. It is Marya that has shed the seeds on the autumnal earth to cover it with Ivan-and-Maryas next year. Marya's job is much more difficult and that is probably why she has wilted sooner than Ivan.

But I am glad that Ivan has weathered the frosts and has even become a deeper blue. I took my last look at this late autumn flower and said softly:

"Ivan, Ivan, where is your Marya?"

The Chase

I had a visitor—Fyodor, a professional hunter from Ramenye. Ramenye is not far from Moscow, just a few hours by train, yet it's still hunting country, where men spend all their winters hunting fox,

---

* The Russian name for wild pansy.

hare, squirrel, and marten. Fyodor, a shoemaker by trade, was one of these men, and though his hunting did not fetch much he was too keen to give it up.

Fyodor had heard that we had a lot of foxes in our parts, and so he came to find out, bringing his hounds along. We knew them well; one was Solovei and the other was called Reston with rather a French sound.

Solovei was a giant of mixed breed: part Kostroma, part borzoi, part plain mongrel—a regular medley resulting in a first-rate hunting dog. When fox-hunting with him you could either use your gun or just pick up the quarry with your bare hands; so long as the fox did not go to earth, Solovei would certainly wear it out and hold it at bay, and, without mauling it, would sit and watch it. The master, on hearing his bark, would come and finish it off. The pups fathered by this dog were plain mongrels by the look of them, but splendid hunting-dogs. They would chase hare, fox, marten, dive into the badger's burrows and follow the animal underground, which laymen always find quite wonderful and even funny for some reason.

Fyodor's breed was quite famous.

Solovei's youngest son was an especially keen dog in his second year of training. But his looks!—you could just see him on a chain in the backyard.

The Moscow hunters were scornful. "That's no dog," they said. "Call him Sharik."* I, too, called this shaggy red-haired mongrel Sharik, not because I was a snob who despised the Fyodor pedigree, but simply because I could not bring myself to call such a democratic-looking dog by his proper name, Ariston.

Some genteel gamekeepers of the landed gentry of old must have suggested the name to Fyodor, but the peasants gave the Greek word new life, like the people of the Renaissance, and later contributed their own reasonable explanation: Reston, they said, was the abbreviation of *rezky ton*, that is, shrill tone.

To continue, on October 7, Fyodor arrived with his Solovei and this red-haired Sharik. All the village hunters who had anything in the shape of a gun came over in the evening and asked us to let them join the hunt next morning. Those who were not hunters took it all very seriously too and begged us to kill a wolf.

The chieftain of this sporting crew was a neighbour of mine, the tinker Tomilin, a man of over forty with a family of nine. One could

---

* A name usually given to mongrels.

not feed such a crowd by soldering samovars or mending pails alone. So he took up making sport guns as a side line, assembling them from all sorts of junk, and proud especially of his wonderful springs.

I enjoy these village hunting parties occasionally, but I always keep a little apart from the rest, because someone's weapon is sure to blow up. Well, no wonder, since the flashing patches of metal brazed to the barrels could be seen with the naked eye. One gun even had its hammer tied down with a piece of string. After a shot, the hammer would fly into the air and dangle on the string, but this did not worry anybody, they did not even mind missing all the time. The main thing was the bang!

I particularly dreaded the blunderbusses, which had not been loaded since last year. At the start of the trip they would be fired to discharge the old cartridge; and when the owner blew through the barrel, the bluish smoke spurted out of it on all sides. Everybody would laugh and say:

"A proper sieve, eh?"

"Give it to your missus to sieve the flour with."

They made fun of themselves, and it was all very jolly and invariably made me think of the days when whole villages went out to hunt the mammoth. Our hunt was even more exciting, to my mind. The mammoth was an awesome beast and everybody had to take him seriously, while our quarry was sometimes nothing more than a white hare hiding under the autumn leaves, a creature no bigger than a large rat. But as for pleasure and cheerful commotion, there were no less of both than in mammoth hunting. It was such fun when one of the huntsmen brandished his gun with the hammer dangling on a piece of string at the invisible mammoth and cried:

"I'll knock your breeches off!"

Now if it had been a real mammoth, somebody would be sure to say, "Mind he doesn't knock yours off instead."

But as it was, they merely said, "Mind your hammer don't hit you in the mug."

And the excitement! Tomilin would get up at two in the morning to see what the weather was like. I would hear him, get up too, and kindle my samovar.

Three o'clock.

Fyodor and I would sit drinking tea. We could see that Tomilin and his son were doing the same. We'd be talking about the hare and the difficulty of tracking it when the leaves were falling.

Four o'clock.

We were still drinking tea, now we talked about the fox and how clever he was, the bastard. Hundreds of examples.

By five o'clock we were debating how best to drive a marten out of a tree hollow. It was best to rub the tree-trunk with a ski, we decided. The marten would think that it was a man climbing up and pop out.

The dull white light of dawn would show in the window. All the hunters would be gathered outside, sitting on the bench and talking quietly.

At last we would get up. We had none of those wet blankets among us who always know beforehand that a thing is hopeless, shuffle along reluctantly somewhere in the rear, and only liven up a little when the adventure turns out a success contrary to their expectation.

Even the heavy dullness of daybreak could not discourage us. What is more, none of us would have exchanged this for the sunrise at some smart villa with the nightingales in song.

It is only in late autumn that one feels so good with the gloom thinning out after the night's rain, the sun breaking through happily, and all the trees shedding their raindrops as if washing themselves.

The woods never stop rustling then, you keep fancying there's someone stealing after you, but there is no need to be afraid, for this is neither friend nor foe, just a preoccupied woodland inhabitant looking for a winter bed.

I saw a snake crawling along slowly and languidly, looking for a quiet spot underground. Unconcerned, it glided on, rustling through the autumn leaves.

The woods had a delicious smell.

One of the hunters said something, or had I just imagined it, mentally adding vigorous human words to the rustle of dying nature? Or perhaps it was the whistling of a restless squirrel? But no, I heard it repeated, and so looked back at my companions.

They were standing very still expecting the hare to fly out of the dense wood at any moment.

Who had spoken those words? Perhaps it was some women picking late mushrooms, and speaking in undertones now and then to break the disturbing murmur of the woods?

"Keep in line, keep in line!"

So this was not the voice of man but of the wild geese calling overhead, pulling one another up.

A vast caravan of geese—too many to count—spread out in the gap between the golden birch tops. I measured fifteen with a stick and moving it along the triangle, reckoned that there must have been over two hundred.

We could hear Solovei barking sporadically in the dense young firs where a hare must have been feeding. The tracks were hard to follow because the night's rain had penetrated even the thicket and washed away part of the traces.

Our huntsmen called the fir coppice the "cupboard" and were sure that the hare was now inside.

"He's scared of the leaves and the dripping. He won't budge from there."

"Sure, he's nailed down now."

"It's not the leaves or the dripping so much. He's lying there because his coat is turning. I saw it myself: his breeches are white, and the rest of him grey."

"Well, if his breeches are white, he won't budge. He's really nailed down in the cupboard."

The trunk of the solitary tall fir-tree in the thicket was covered with creamy resin and the whole of the cupboard was carpeted with dead birch leaves, while more of them kept falling, whispering softly.

"A regular cupboard it is," said one of our hunters, yawning.

Tinker Tomilin yawned too.

Did anyone think we would yawn on this hunt when we started out?

"Can't we go and help Solovei?" said Tomilin.

Everyone gave the cupboard a speculative look as if measuring it to see if one would get through or stick.

And suddenly we all got up and decided to go and help Solovei. Yelling, we charged at the cupboard, the soldered patches on the mended barrels flashing in the sun. Tomilin, who took the lead, tore straight through the saplings yelling, and the more he was pricked, the more he yelled. Everybody was yelling, hissing, squealing and yelping. Their voices sounded differently now, this was probably a throwback to the days when men hunted the mammoth.

There was a shot, and a wild shout: here goes!

The first and hardest part of the hunt was over. It had been like a fuse smoldering under a barrel of powder for a whole hour before it finally exploded.

"He's off!" roared everybody exultantly. "He's off!"

Solovei was baying steadily and confidently and then Sharik joined in. His tone was indeed very shrill.

In a twinkling the whole crowd of young men dashed helter-skelter through the thick undergrowth to head off the quarry, and Tomilin, shedding his years, went crashing through the brush like an elk.

No hare was ever headed off that way, but who cared as long as they could tear madly through the woods like greyhounds!

Fyodor and I, two old-timers, exchanged knowing glances and smiled, listening to the chase. We guessed where the hare was likely to break out and took our posts: Fyodor in the clearing opposite the cupboard door, and I a little farther off, where three grassy paths crossed between the tall coppice and the thick bushes.

No sooner did the sound of the forty-year-old tinker crashing through the bushes die away, than I saw the flickering white breeches along a green path far ahead between the forest and the shrubbery, and then the hare in person, hoppety-hopping straight at me.

I watched him over the sights of my gun; my mammoth was a small white hare of the late autumn sort. He had his enormous ears at one end of his very short body and his long legs at the other, legs so long that he bobbed up and down as he ran.

I was faced with the grave responsibility of keeping the mammoth from getting back into the cupboard so the dogs should not get stuck there again. I simply had to kill this mammoth. I took aim.

He squatted.

I never shoot at a sitting animal, but his end was inevitable anyway: if he ran towards me the sights were on his front paws, if he jumped aside they would move to his head.

The poor mammoth was doomed.

But suddenly—

A ginger head, greyish from the heavy dew, popped from the thicket.

"Sharik?"

I nearly shot him, taking him for a fox. But it *was* a fox, it wasn't Sharik at all.

The rest happened in a flash. The head had no time to move forward or hide. I fired and the rusty bundle toppled over in the tall grass, while the white breeches flickered far away.

The dogs came flying. . . .

Fyodor came flying. Tomilin with his gun atilt as in a charge dashed out of the wood followed by the rest, their patched guns flashing. Held on the leash the dogs struggled to get at the fox, barking in a frenzy. All the men were yelling, trying to outshout one another that he, too, had seen the fox as it streaked through the underbrush. When the dogs cooled down and the young men grew quieter, we all became aware of a happiness which, affecting us in equal measure, blended us into one.

"It's a cried-up fox," Fyodor said.

"It's a cracked-up fox," Tomilin put in.

Anchar

I like hounds but hate halooing, shouting, trudging through the brush, and in general acting like a dog myself. The way I used to enjoy hunting best was letting the dog loose while I made myself some tea, never hurrying even when the dog was stalking the quarry. I just sat there drinking my tea and listening. And when the time came I got up and went straight to the spot—bang!—and that was all there was to it.

That is what I call good hunting.

I once had a dog called Anchar I could do it with. Today a tree-stump marks his grave in Alexeyevo Sech, where a gully leads to the clearing.

I did not rear him. He was brought to me by a peasant—a full-grown, well-knit dog with circles around the eyes.

"Stolen?" I asked.

"Yes," he said. "But it was a long time ago. My son-in-law stole him from the kennels when he was a pup. But that needn't worry you. He's a pure breed alright."

"Never mind about breeds, just tell me how is he at chasing?"

"He's fine."

We went out for a try. We had hardly left the village when he set the dog free, and it was gone in a flash, leaving just a green trail in the greyish grass.

"I'm a bit cold," said the peasant when we were in the woods. "What about lighting a fire?"

"What nonsense," I thought, "he must be pulling my leg."

But no, he was quite serious. He went about gathering sticks, he lit the fire and sat down.

"And what about the dog?" I asked.

"You're young, and I'm old," he said. "You've never seen anything like this, but now you shall. Don't worry about the dog—he knows his job. He's been told to look about while we're having tea," he grinned.

We had a cup each.

The dog gave voice and I started up.

But the old peasant only laughed and poured himself another cup. "Let's hear what he's after first."

We listened. He was barking loudly in hot and fast pursuit.

"He's chasing a fox," said the peasant.

We had another cup each while the dog must have covered four versts or so. Suddenly the barking was cut short.

"Are your cows out there?" he asked, pointing.

He was right: the Karachunovo villagers usually grazed their cows there.

"The fox's lured him on to the trail of the cows. Now he'll have to pick it up again. Let's have another cup."

But the fox was only allowed a short respite. The dog soon picked up its tracks afresh and began to range in narrow circles—clearly it was a local fox. The peasant emptied his cup into the fire and stamped out the embers.

"And now we've got to hurry," he said.

We rushed to the fox-holes in the clearing, to head off the chase. We had just got ready when we saw it in the clearing with the dog practically at its tail. It tried to mislead the dog into the bog by waving its tail, but the hound knew better and flew straight for its neck— and it was all over. There lay the fox with the dog at its side licking a paw.

The dog had a stupid name, he was called Gonchar, but in my excitement I shouted: "Anchar."*

And so the name stuck. I always called him Anchar.

Do you know how a hunter's heart unfolds? Picture a morning when the frost lies on the grass and there's a thin mist before dawn, receding slowly as the sun comes up, and instead of the mist there's a blueness now between the green firs and the golden birches, and on and on it goes, a clearer blue, a brighter gold, a merrier sparkle. This is how a grim October day unfolds and that is just the way a hunter's heart unfolds too: a good gulp of cold and sun, a head-clearing sneeze, and every man he meets becomes a friend.

"My friend," I said to the peasant. "What misfortune is making you sell this fine dog to a stranger?"

"I know he'll be in good hands," he said. "As for my misfortune, it's the usual thing. My cow ate some frozen grass, swelled up, and

---

* Gonchar means "potter," and Anchar "upas-tree," well known in Russia from Pushkin's poem.

died. I have to buy another—a peasant can't do without a cow."

"I know, and I'm sorry for you. How much do you want for the dog?"

"Just a cow. You have two, so give me your spotted one."

And so I bartered a cow for Anchar.

Ah, what an autumn I had! No halooing, no scrambling through bushes, but just strolling about and admiring the deepening gold of the trees, or then again I would stamp out some paths for the hazel-hens, imitate their call and they would come running to me along these paths. But then the golden season was over. One particularly frosty morning the sun rose bright and warm and by midday the last leaves dropped from the trees. The hazel-hen no longer answered my decoy call. Then came the rains, the leaves began to rot, November was there—the saddest month of the year.

I'm not keen on going hunting in a gang; I like to walk through the forest slowly and quietly, stopping and catching my breath, and then all woodland creatures take me for one of themselves. I love observing all living things, I marvel at them all and only kill what I should. There is nothing I hate more than a gang crashing through the woods, yelling and shouting and firing at everything that comes their way. It is different with a good friend and skillful hunter, who asks me to take him along. It is not the same sort of pleasure, of course, but pleasure it is in its own way. I love good company. Well then, a friend of mine wrote to me from Moscow early in November asking if he could come and go hunting with me. There is no need to give his name. I wrote that I would be glad to have him. And so he turned up on the evening of the sixth of that dull November.

As it happened, there had been a spell of fine crisp weather, but the thaw set in that very day, the ground was all muddy, and there was an unbroken chilly drizzle. I could not sleep that night for worry that the tracks would be washed away in the rain. But the stars broke out just after midnight and by morning the hares had made plenty of footprints for us.

We drank our tea and had a good talk before dawn as the morning stars came out, and when the window was streaked with grey we set out with Anchar for hares.

The fields of winter rye that autumn came close up to the village and the young stalks were so thick and strong and lusciously green that one felt one could almost eat them oneself. The hares had been feasting on them till the fat hung inside them like grapes—I used to get as much as a pound of fat from a hare. Anchar caught the scent briskly, circled round a bit and set off straight for the hare's lair. There was a continuous rustling and dripping in the woods. The hare, scared by this, was apt to come out and settle in the clearing opposite Alexeyevo Sech. As I understood Anchar, he made for the clearing from the ryefields, anxious to get to the waste ground near the gully because the hares, when scared off from the clearing, were sure to go that way. I posted my friend on the edge of the gully and took the other side myself where he could not see me while I saw him perfectly.

One has to form a plan when hunting too, but one can seldom carry it out. We waited and waited but Anchar neither gave voice nor showed up, he had simply vanished.

"Seryozha!" I shouted.

Well, I did not mean to give you his name, but there are plenty of Seryozhas about.

"Seryozha!" I shouted. "Call Anchar!"

I had lent him my hunting horn because he could blow it very well and loved doing it. He had just lifted the horn when I saw Anchar running up the gully. I could tell by the way he ran that he was on the same tracks as before, but the hare must have been scared up by a fox or an owl and had already passed the gully, and now Anchar was in hot pursuit. As soon as Anchar came level with my friend, he raised his gun and took aim.

Disaster would have been averted had I remembered just then that once at this very spot I myself had taken aim at a man and very nearly shot him: he had been walking up the gully wearing a hareskin cap and that was all I could see of him. I had been just about to press the trigger when the rest of the head appeared. Had my memory flashed me a warning I would have realized that only a bit of the animal's coat could be seen from above, and would have shouted to stop him. But I thought he was fooling—those city hunters often behave like restive horses after a long spell in the stable.

I thought he was fooling, when suddenly—bang.

It grew very still; the gully was hidden behind a smoke screen.

My heart sank, and instantly I remembered how I had nearly shot that man.

The bluish smoke settled in the green gully, I stood waiting and the seconds passed like years and there was no Anchar. No—he did not appear out of the smoke. And when it cleared away I saw him sleeping on the green grass as on his mat—asleep for ever.

Heavy mournful drops were falling from the tall trees to the shorter ones, from the shorter ones to the bushes, from the bushes to the grass, their sad whispering growing softer and softer and dying away as it reached the ground: and the ground absorbed the tears in complete silence.

I looked down, dry-eyed.

"Well," I thought, "it might be worse. People, too, get shot by accident sometimes."

I am a hardened man, I soon pulled myself together and even thought how best to comfort my friend, because he must have felt no better than I: weren't we both hunters and didn't we know how to drown our sorrow? There was a still in every cottage in Tsiganovo, and I decided we'd go there and wash down our grief. I was thinking this, but as I watched my friend across the gully I wondered. He came down, looked at the dead Anchar, and returned to his post, as if he were still waiting for him to give voice.

What was he up to?

"Hello," I shouted.

He shouted in reply.

"What did you shoot at?"

He was silent.

"What were you shooting at?" I repeated.

"At an owl," he said.

My heart shrank.

"Did you hit it?"

"No, I missed," he answered.

I sat down on a rock and suddenly understood.

"Seryozha," I shouted.

"Well?"

"Blow the horn for Anchar."

He picked up the horn, but did not blow it. He took a step in my direction—he must have been ashamed of himself—then another step and stopped to think.

"Come on!" I shouted.

He raised the horn again.

"Hurry up, will you!"

He put the horn to his lips.

"Come on!"

He began to blow. I sat on the rock and listened and thought all sorts of silly thoughts: there was a crow chasing a hawk. I wondered why the hawk did not knock it on the head instead—once would have been enough. With thoughts like these, you can sit on a stone for ever. All the time a vital question preyed on my mind: Why need people lie? Death is the end, everything ends so simply, so why don't people leave it at that? But no, there was my dog shot, our sport over, he had shot the dog himself and he knew that I was man enough to say nothing about it to him and not to reproach him in any way, and yet. . . .

Whom was he trying to deceive?

"I tell you what," I said. "You go along that path over there until you come to Tsiganovo and we'll have a drink there. Just go on blowing the horn, and I'll walk about here and listen in case Anchar replies."

"Perhaps you'd better take the horn and blow it yourself?"

"No," I said. "If I do the blowing I shan't hear a thing and I've got to listen to the least sound."

"But where are you going?" he asked timidly.

I pointed in the direction where Anchar lay. Surely I had him cornered, he'd have to own up to it now, I thought. But no, he didn't.

"I shouldn't go that way," he said. "There aren't any trees there; the dog can't hang itself on a bush, can it?"

"All right," I said. "I'll go the other way. But don't you forget to keep blowing as you go. Just go on and on and blow as you go."

He brightened up when I said I would go the other way and went off blowing the horn, blowing and blowing for three versts.

"No," I said to myself as he went away. "There may be many miracles at the birth of life but none at the death. Anchar will not reply and a real sportsman would look me straight in the eye and say, 'Come and have a drink my friend—it's all over.' "

Truly, whom was he trying to deceive?

I always carried a small hatchet in my belt just in case. I cut down a bough, shaped it into a spade of sorts and dug a hole in the soft ground. I laid my good Anchar in it, covered him with earth and bordered the grave with turf. In the burnt-out clearing, I remembered, there was that twisted, charred stump which always frightened the women who took it for a wood sprite in the twilight. I dragged this stump to the grave and set it up as a tombstone.

I stood there looking at the wood sprite while Seryozha kept blowing the horn. Seryozha, whom are you trying to deceive?

There was a chilly drizzle. Heavy mournful drops fell from the tall trees to the shorter ones, from the shorter ones to the bushes, from the bushes to the grass and from the grass to the damp earth. The whole wood was whispering, whispering, "Dash it, dash it, dash it. . . ."

But mother earth accepted all the tears in silence and drank them up, drank them all up.

I felt as if all the roads in the world converged, and the end of the way was where my wood sprite stood over a dog's grave, staring at me so solemnly.

"Listen," I said. "Listen, you wood sprite."

And I delivered an oration, but what I said then I shall not reveal.

I felt easier after that and walked on to Tsiganovo.

"Stop blowing the horn, Seryozha," I said. "It's all over, I know everything—whom are you trying to deceive?"

He turned very pale.

We had a few drinks together and spent the night in Tsiganovo. You all know this man, every one of us has his own Seryozha to remember.

WINTER

The Death Run

I've had to tramp the woods in winter in the past; I've had my fill of frosts. And even now whenever I look at the grey blur of woods in the twilight I always feel ill at ease. But in the crisp morning after a fresh snowfall I go to the woods well before sunrise and celebrate my own private Christmas more gloriously than anyone has ever done, it seems to me.

I was not given long enough to admire the snowy palaces and listen to the deep silence that day. My foxhound Solovei soon gave the signal. Like the famous Solovei-the-Robber,* he first hissed, whistled, and then bayed, shattering the silence. He always made those queer sounds when he picked up a fresh track.

While he was following the track I hurried towards the clearing with the three firs, where the fox usually passed, and halted behind the green screen, watching through the gaps. Now he was chasing it, coming nearer and nearer.

The fox sprang into the clearing from a coppice of fir-trees quite far away, a red flash on white, looking very much like a dog except for its beautiful and apparently useless tail. A grin seemed to flicker across its angry mask, the splendid tail flashed, and the lovely vixen was gone.

Solovei dashed out from the coppice, red-coated like her, strong and utterly wild: he had all but gone stark mad the day he saw the tracks of the cunning beauty on the white for the first time, and since then during the chase he acted more like a wild ferocious beast than the good-natured dog he was. Niether horn nor gunshot could call him off. He ran oblivious of everything, howling with all his might,

---

* A fabulous robber of the Russian epic songs. He could whistle so loudly that this alone caused death.

determined to get or die. His frenzy was so infectious that I often found myself coming to my senses at the fall of darkness some eight versts from home, in the snowy heart of a strange forest.

The footprints of the dog and the fox wove in and out around the clearing. In the thicket the dog went by scent until he saw the track, crossed the clearing and picked it up by the little fir-tree where the vixen had shown me her tail. There still some hope that she was a local animal and would return in narrowing circles. But soon the barking failed from earshot and did not come back. The fox was a stranger and had gone home.

Now my chase began. I had to follow the trail until I heard the dog give voice again. Mostly the tracks wove along the edges of the forest clearings, the fox circling and the dog cutting across. I also tried to take the shortest possible cuts. I saw nothing but the tracks and all my thoughts were on them alone. Like Solovei I was a maniac that day and ready for anything.

Suddenly, there was a perfect maze of tracks, mostly of hares, but with the fox's interwoven. The vixen had tried a double ruse. She had meant to conceal her own tracks and at the same time try and tempt Solovei astray with the fresh tracks of the hares. Her ruse succeeded at first. The tracks were so fresh that surely the hare must be lying right under the nearest bush, blinking its brilliant button eyes. Solovei had dashed astray. Could he have left the vixen to follow the wretched little hare?

Her track had parted from that of the hare, passed into the marshes round the edge of a clump of young aspens, which had been gnawed by hares, and—hello—here were Solovei's heavy tracks, running out of the wood. And the tracks of the two had joined in the final death run.

I thought I heard Solovei's howl. I stopped to listen: I must have imagined it. The silence was complete, but I fancied I heard the faint whistling of hazel-hens. The tracks came out in the fields, the sun made them look blue—a blue animal path running across the vast field.

The lithe fox had dived under the low stakes of a fence, which the dog could not do. He had tried to jump over, and the snow on the top showed two dents made by his mighty paws. Now I knew that I had not been mistaken: the dog had howled to complain that he had fallen off the fence and had had to make a detour. I could not see where he had got round it, but at the edge of the firebreak I came upon new tracks twisted together and running into difficult grounds.

There was no trial more bitter for a hunter than this firebreak. Once upon a time the heated ground had caught fire, raising huge clumsy hillocks and felling the trees one over another, where they still lay in haphazard tiers, thickly overgrown. This made hard going for a fox, let alone a dog or a man. The fox had run in there to throw him off her tracks without meaning to stay long. She had dived under a tree, leaving a tunnel, while the dog leapt over the log, brushing off some snow and obliterating a polecat's footprint on it. Misled by the deceptive fluffy surface, they both fell into a deep pit. The vixen darted up the second tier of logs, and on to the third, and ran along a log as far as the middle, while the dog balanced himself for a while, and then tumbled down. I could hear somebody chopping firewood nearby, and, whoever it was, he must have been having a good view of the animals leaping and falling one after the other. But I could not possibly follow their route. I made a detour round the firebreak, frightfully sorry that I could not run with them.

I failed to find the tracks emerging from the firebreak, but suddenly heard a long plaintive howl from the direction of the state woods. I rushed straight towards the sound to help the chase, though I was out of breath and as hot as if I were in the tropics.

I need not have troubled. Solovei had put himself right and was already out of earshot again. But I absolutely had to find out why he had howled so long and so plaintively. A broad road ran through the state wood. The vixen had probably struck the road and a sledge, coming along soon after, had driven over the fresh tracks. Perhaps it was this very sledge that was now coming back—the decorated sledge carrying red-nosed matchmakers with frost-covered beards on their way to fetch more wine. Solovei had run out into the road in hot pursuit, but this was not the forest where he knew everything from his ancestors, the wolves, far better than we humans did. The road had come much later, and was an alien country to him. This straight man-made line was bewildering in its terrifying infinity. At first he started in the wrong direction—from where the matchmakers had come. He had run for some time, looking for the tracks, and was at last so frightened by the endlessness of the road that he squatted and howled calling upon man to explain to him the secret of the road. He kept howling all the time I was blundering about the firebreak.

Then he must have turned and run blindly in the other direction until he stumbled upon a mark left by the fox's tail and took heart. Further on the fox had dashed aside but had not liked it for some reason and came back leaving a half-circle of prints. Solovei followed these until they became obliterated by the matchmakers returning with the wine.

I might not have noticed where the vixen had dashed into the bushes but for Solovei plunging after her with all his weight and making a hollow in the snow. Further along I could see the tracks running side by side in a race of life and death, sweeping the white caps from the black tree-stumps.

They had not gone in a straight line for long—animals do not care for straight lines. They again flew across country from field to field and meadow to meadow.

I saw with satisfaction that once the fox had tried to rest and marked the spot.

Were anyone to ask me now I could not for the life of me tell just where I caught up with the narrowing circles of the chase. I remember only that there was a grove of tall pines which gave way abruptly to a small thicket with wide clear patches. The tracks criss-crossed several times in every clearing. It was there I heard Solovei's urgent baying: the circles were narrowing. My guesswork was over, I was no longer a pathfinder, I now entered this mad contest as its third, most terrible participant.

Snow flakes had settled lavishly on my gun and as I brushed them off I knew from the way my finger stung how bitter the frost was. From behind the small fir I saw, in the slanting rays of the sun, the vixen steal through the thicket, her mouth gaping. The snow crunched loudly now in the frost but it did not worry me, the fox was too exhausted to try a long dash and was sure to meet me on one of its narrow circles.

She ventured out into the open and ran across the clearing to my fir, her tongue lolling to one side, but her eyes still burning evilly, her malice masked with her customary grin. My hands were tingling from the cold, but even if they were to freeze to the barrels, I would not have let her escape. Solovei took a short cut and catching sight of her made a plunge. The vixen met him seated, her sharp white teeth and grin turned upon his ferocious and kindest of faces. He had been nipped by such sharp teeth more than once and had been ill for weeks afterwards. He could not go for her face to face but only if she took flight again. And this was by no means the end yet. She had yet another ruse for him: a wave of her handsome tail to mislead him while she dived into the young firs. And it was getting dark.

He was howling. They were breathing almost into each other's muzzles. Both were covered with frost, the steam from their breath turning instantly into crystals.

I had a hard job stealing up over the crunching snow: the frost must have been fierce indeed. But the fox was beyond all hearing now, baring her sharp teeth in her everlasting evil grin. Solovei must not take notice of me either. If he did and bounded forward, she would have him by the throat. Unheeded by either, I watched them from behind a fir branch, and I did not have far to go now.

The last ray of the wintry sun touched the tall pines, setting the trunks ablaze for a moment, and then the lights went out like so many Christmas candles. Nor was there any gentle voice to say:

"May peace be with you, my dear beasts."

Grandfather Frost cracked a nut somewhere and the sound was as loud as a shot in the forest.

Suddenly all was confusion. The handsome tail flashed in the air and Solovei darted aside, misled by the ruse. My gun cracked, only it was not a snapping sound like Grandfather Frost's, but a long one, bouncing from tree to tree.

The vixen played dead, but I saw her lay back her ears. Solovei made a leap. She sank her teeth into his cheek. I beat her off with a stick, and now he sank his teeth into her back. I put my foot on her neck and struck her with my knife. She was dead but her teeth were still clenched on my felt boots. I had to pry them open with the barrel of my gun.

I always felt ashamed when I came to my senses after the madness of a chase as I slung a wretched limp hare over my shoulder, but this queen of the woods was no anti-climax to a hunt even when dead, and Solovei would have gone worrying the carcass if I had let him.

The shadows had already deepened into twilight.

The Heart of Winter

I came to live on a hill by the shore of the largest lake in central Russia, in an empty house supposedly haunted by demons guarding the treasures hidden in the hill. I had only meant to stay the summer, but some geographers, very queer people, who came along to study the lake, talked me into spending the winter there.

Geographers are mostly queer people I have noticed, or at any rate not like the rest of us who live our lives as though the earth were flat and immobile. They lead a ship-board existence, for ever sailing round the sun, so naturally they see our world quite differently.

These young people were all a bit eccentric, though their leader, a middle-aged grey professor, vigorous and tireless, did not at all look like a geographer and was a cheerful and perfectly normal man. He and I decided to set up a geographical post in my house and I consented to take on the job of observer and caretaker. Before they left, the students moved all their geographical instruments and devices into my room, and the professor promised to come back in a week's time to bring the documents endorsing my appointment, direct me in my observations and instruct me in the use of the instruments. That was in July, but though winter was already well under way, the professor had not come, and the instruments lay gathering dust in a corner of my room. So the professor turned out to be a true geographer after all.

As I waited for his return I began to make various observations after my own fashion. I decided that since geography interested me primarily in as much as it helped to train one to think of life in terms of motion, it would not matter very much whether I made my observations in a strictly scientific manner or just jotted down all the daily changes in the appearance of the sun, the moon, the lake, nature generally, and man living close to nature. After all, my observations would record the changes day by day as stages in the movement of our planet. I even worked out a method of my own, trying to make vivid and accurate notes of the passing days. I floundered for some weeks, which is inevitable in any new undertaking, but gradually I got into my stride, and soon really felt I was on a voyage aboard the planet Earth.

I jotted down little things just as they occurred to me, for though they might appear trifling today, they might add up tomorrow to form a picture of the planet's voyage. While only yesterday the ant-hill kingdom had teemed with life, today its subjects had retired to the depths of their state, and we sat resting on their ant-hill as safely as in a chair. Yesterday we were sledging along the edge of the lake, listening to the talk of the swans in the ice-free pool, and in the wintry silence it sounded to us as if some highly intelligent creatures were holding a grave conference. Today the swans flew off and we deciphered their talk of yesterday—they had been holding council about their migration. I noted down thousands of touching details accompanying the voyage of our planet revolving around the sun: the black water filled with icy needles tinkling as it washed against the ice-bound inlets, the bits of floating ice sparkling on a sunlit day, the late gulls mistaking them for fish, and the night the lake grew utterly silent with the telephone wires alone humming over the dead valley which only yesterday had teemed with life in all its complexity.

I was no longer sorry I had agreed to stay the winter and was not particularly annoyed with the geographer for not showing me how to use his instruments. Expensive apparatus was not available to all, but what I did was: I was paving the way for all those scattered over the length and breadth of the vast country, brought up on a flat earth and languishing immobile in their narrow vision. It takes no more than ten minutes to describe the features of the day, and in a few months you can build up a new picture of the motion of life, a unique picture for life never repeats itself and our voyage round the sun is different each year.

Frost is sometimes born in the hour before daybreak. The strength and direction of the wind are then defined and if you want to know what the day will be like you have to go out of doors and watch for the coming of dawn. I only had twenty paces to go from my house to the sheer cliff overhanging the lake, and there I would stand watching the slender twigs of the aspen chasing one another across the disc of the moon. This aspen was like the fleece of the earth in which I was hidden, and the twigs the strands of wool, revealing the movement of our planet by passing across the disc—my favourite test and probably the only way to see this movement with the naked eye. It was easy to forget the false ideas of childhood about the flat motionless earth as I stood there in the empty hour before dawn, feeling like a passenger on an enormous ship with his own bearings of latitude and longitude. Yes, I was the passenger now, but in ages to come my own spirit, transferred to another through thousands of lives, will navigate this ship from the dying sun to a warmer star.

An onslaught of wind shook the aspen and disrupted the visible movement, but whether I saw it or not my planet was still on its course through space. The wind grew stronger and the trees tapped each other with their frozen branches. As day broke the temperature fell half a degree every ten minutes, until the future captain of the earth had to leave the bridge: fifteen below with a strong wind. The sun sent forth flashes of crimson swords.

I went back to the house to kindle the samovar and when I returned five minutes later, the swords were gone, the sun was hidden, and the surface of the lake was swept by whirls of snow, laying bare patches of dark ice. Before the night's tracks of the animals were drifted over, I skied off to see if the wolf had visited the grave of my dog again, and soon found the familiar footprints in the bushes mixed with those of a fox. Both had come and had gnawed at the bones. The wolf must have been very old because he kept aloof of the pack. It's a rule with them: once they grow old and their teeth decay so they cannot keep up with the youngsters, they have to shift for themselves. Such a wolf is mainly on the look-out for dogs, and the hunters call him a dog-wolf. This cursed dog-wolf worried the life out of me every time my Solovei, chasing a fox, got out of earshot.

"You just wait, my good sir, I'll treat you to a bit of lead soon enough," I said studying the tracks. From the gully they went into the field where the wind had powdered them with snow, turning them into little knobs, with toes and claws moulded so perfectly they looked like plaster casts. I followed the knobs for a while, but the capricious blizzard seemed to have suddenly decided to stop my inquiry and wiped them out completely.

As I walked back I thought of the fox's tracks and tried to follow them just in case: in a blizzard the gully was a very comfortable place for the fox to lie in. I walked the circle counting the incoming and outgoing tracks, but to the very last step, closing the circle, I could not tell whether the fox was in the gully or not. Finally, there was only a juniper bush between me and the spot where my circle began, and my heart beat faster. I rounded the bush and saw no outgoing track: the circle was complete—I had learned one of the secrets of the neighbourhood and discovered that within this circle slept the voracious enemy of my woodcock and partridges.

Now I could visualize the story of the fox's night raids. Last night it had chased the black grouse I had spared that summer in order to hear their mating songs in the spring from my front porch. There were six of them, two grey hens and four cocks with red crests and lyre-like tails. The snow was piled so high they could reach the branches of the juniper bushes from below. They had wandered round all day, leaving the long lovely chains of their footprints between the bushes. Towards evening they had burrowed in the snow, each of them making a comfortable hole with a little window at the top for breathing. In the dusk the fox must have picked up their tracks, stolen to their bedrooms, along the chain of their tracks, and pulled one of the cocks out. There was a heap of feathers on the snow and traces of blood. The fox had had a good supper and curled up on a flat table-like hummock of moss under a tablecloth of snow. The supper was so filling that it did not go for its morning prowl, but there was even more likelihood it was the blizzard that stopped it.

The fox was fast asleep, unaware that two hunters were conspiring against its life. After arguing in whispers we decided to take advantage of the strong wind and narrow the circle. We each took a reel of cord and marked the circle, attaching little red flags to the cord stretched from one bush to the next. We went in different directions and where we met the magic circle closed. We were triumphant, for once the fox was beflagged it was as good as in the bag.

We could have kept it in that circle for three days or more if we liked: for all its animal cunning it lacks that grain of human common sense or, for that matter, a lynx's or even a bear's to see through the hunters' ruse and just leap over the cord.

We took down a length of cord in front of a small but very bushy fir behind which it would be easy to hide—making an exit for the fox. One of us stood just behind the fir with his gun ready, loaded with twenty-four slugs dipped in paraffin to keep from scattering. The other entered the circle from the opposite side, stepping carefully along the ingoing tracks, whistling from time to time softly or snapping a frozen twig.

The fox was still asleep, never suspecting that the chain of flags had closed in on it except for one fatal exit. But its sense of hearing is alert even in sleep. It heard the whistle and raised its head. A twig snapped. It got up and listened again, then moved on cautiously.

"Keep back! The flags!"

It drew back, afraid.

"Keep back! The flags!"

It squatted and listened. A twig snapped very close. In leaps and bounds the fox made straight for the fatal exit.

The hands of a watch would sooner stick together than my black sights waver from that red flank.

One may hunt by rule and one may hunt by hazard. I hunt mostly by rule and live by hazard: somehow I have never been able to arrange things properly, for life is short, it's a pity to lose time and energy on trifles. No sensible man would drift into the deep of winter and only then remember that he had put in no stocks of firewood, or reduce his purse to a mere sixteen kopeks in cash before the need to do something about it occurred to him. But I have lived by hazard many a year and have learned how to meet exigencies when they came: the main thing is to be cheerful. It is not always easy, but what else can one do if one cannot live by rule?

Well then, I had burned my last pile of firewood but instead of worrying about it I went out hunting and returned with a fox. People

saw me carrying it, and before we had time to skin it, down came a
buyer who offered me enough for that skin to buy a good supply of
the best birch firewood. I then sent word to my best friend, Uncle
Mikhei, to get me the wood as soon as he could.

A storm raged all night and by morning the house was icy. I went
out to make my observations before dawn but came back immediately.
There was nothing to record: only a howling and whistling and a
frost biting you to the marrow. Meanwhile Uncle Mikhei, after a
substantial meal, must have wrapped himself up well, and gone out
for my firewood. Bagging such a heap of firewood with a single shot
was a stroke of luck he would never have. He was not absent-minded,
he lived by rule and stocked his firewood in the summer. He sold
firewood for a living, and regarded it as an important public duty
that provided others with fuel and him with a living. The dry wood
was for sale and the damp wood for his own use, and so his cottage
was always cold. The only warm place was the stove. There was just
enough room on the stove-bed for his wife and children, while Uncle
Mikhei had to sleep outside it. But I refuse to understand this sort
of living by rule, and prefer to live by hazard, doing my best not to
wrong others.

At dawn it was still blowing a bit: it just tickled my nose and my
skis sank two feet deep in the snow-drifts. When I looked at my house
it was a house no longer, but Nansen's *Fram* trapped in the ice of the
Arctic with the wide seething ocean all around and no human dwelling
in sight, not a trace of man anywhere, not even a track of a wild
animal. The old woman would certainly be unable to bring the milk
from the village. And Uncle Mikhei would spare his nag and himself
too—the nag came first naturally. What should I do? I put on the
warmest clothes I had, took my hatchet and went into the forest to
get myself something in the way of firewood. The juniper bushes
were piled up with rugged dunes of snow. I sank into one of them
to the neck, and my hands went numb while I floundered in it. And
all at once everything was veiled in white from earth to sky, as if some
enormous white hunter were beflagging me with a white cord.

Everything seems strangely magnified in a blizzard. The bushes
seemed like a tall forest, and suddenly a monster with ears a yard
long leaped out and flew straight for me. I swung my hatchet to
defend myself, but the hare must have been more terrified than I
was, for he swerved and vanished. A moment later I saw the thing
that must have scared the hare up: it was a tall white tower, and Uncle
Mikhei spoke from inside it, saying in a very ordinary voice:

"If I'd had a stick in my hand, I'd have killed the cross-eyed rascal."
It was true: he killed more hares with a stick than with a gun.
"And what about my firewood, Uncle Mikhei?"
"I've tipped it out."

He had got stuck and unloaded it somewhere in the field. We made several trips there and back with our small sledge, and got all the stoves going. Smoke streamed from every chimney of my *Fram*, dissolving in the infinite white as easily as the smoke of a cigarette.

When the room was more or less warm I sat down to record my observations. That white splendour we had had till then and which we called winter, I saw as a mere foretaste of it. It was only now that we had reached the heart of winter. And it made me fancy that the white hunter was beflagging us, leaving a single fatal exit for every one of us. What should we do? Sympathy and pity for man gives way to wintry grimness in the struggle for life.

And the stove was burning brighter and hotter.

Turn of the Sun

As countless as the pure white flakes that fell from the sky that snowy winter were the obscene curses that fell from the lips of the peasants carting timber from the depths of the Pereslavl-Zalessky District to the station of Berendeyevo. And the more it snowed, the more they cursed whenever they met, for each wanted to drive the horses of his fellow into the drifts and not his own.

When in a good mood I took no notice of the carters' bad language, but just continued measuring the depth of the snow or the ice on the lake, making notes of each new happening in the life of nature and drawing conclusions about the movement of the earth, and then I really felt I was on a voyage round the sun aboard the ship called Earth. I noticed something new every day, training my eye to mark the constant motion of life, which never repeats itself.

But when something unpleasant happened in my private cabin or I felt out of sorts and could not admire the drifting soft flakes, I would hear nothing but the peasants' curses growing in volume and force. This, too, was a gauge that showed that the snow was falling thicker, which added also to the picture of continuous motion: whether one looked up into the sky or down at the ground, we were moving.

We have all been brought up to think of life as going on on a motionless plain and to ignore the dizzy flight of our planet in our daily existence. We soon forget all the geography we learned at school as being of no practical value in our daily routine. I thought much about it, and it seemed to me that my work of recording and summarizing the characteristics of each movement would have tremendous importance if I could impart the feeling of this movement to man brought up on the notion of the motionless plain. I would call my voyage aboard the Earth the "All Year Round."

A boy sent by the village schoolteacher brought me the *Izvestiya*.

"What holiday have we tomorrow?" I asked him.

"A Soviet holiday."

"Christmas is a Christian festival," I said. "Why should it be Soviet?"

"So what?"

"What do you mean, so what? Are you going to celebrate it in your village?"

"No, they don't want to celebrate our Christmas and we don't want to celebrate theirs."

"Who do you mean by they, you funny boy?"

I told him about the movement of the earth and tomorrow's equinox, the great festival of the Turn of the Sun, which meant an increase of light and perhaps an increase of wisdom. He had heard it all at school and was not interested in more geography: the earth could go on flying and the light increasing, but still they would make merry.

"He is right," I thought. "I shall succeed only if I make geography as enjoyable as merry making."

I at once made a note that I had to make my voyage around the sun sound fascinating.

There was a blizzard that night, and when I went into the yard once or twice it was still blowing furiously. The wolf-hunt we planned for tomorrow seemed quite out of the question. But as it happened a pair of old wolves had lingered till daybreak busy with the meat planted for them. Somebody had frightened them off in the early hours of the morning; they had come out into the middle of the lake and halted, wondering where to turn next. The leader of our wolf-hunt, the giant Fedya, and his chief assistant, Dmitry Nikolayevich, the cashier from the local bank, had spotted them, and when the pair moved in the wrong direction, they had headed them off and driven them into our wood. The beasts were full, and disinclined to run far. They came to rest near the village behind the carrion dumping ground.

I had gone with Fedya to flag in the wolves in the deep snow before. It all but killed me trying to keep pace with the giant. I'd collapse, lapping at the snow like a dog, with the steam fairly rising from me, but the giant would just call me chicken-hearted and prod me with a ski for good measure. I had enough of flagging with him and now joined the party as one of the shots.

I was sure the hunt was off that day, and suddenly a boy came to fetch me.

"The wolves are flagged."

That means that a circle of flags has closed in on the wolves and the shooting can begin. Whenever a hunter hears that the wolves are flagged, he drops everything and hurries to the spot because the winter day is short. There were no horses to be had anywhere because the peasants were all carting timber; the boy had come in what was almost a child's sledge driven by a colt. But we drove along smartly enough until we were held up by a train of timber carts which seemed to us a verst long as, plunged in the snowy sea, we waited for them to pass. Then we met another, and again it was some versts long, and the day was drawing to a close. That is one of the main snags in wolf-hunting: the shortness of the day. But we got to the village when it was still light, with only a verst to go to the marshes, and all would be well unless we met another timber train.

And what with our time getting so short we came up against a new snag.

"Off you get," the owner of the colt and sledge told us.

"What d'you mean?"

"Our deal was the village and back."

That is what always happens in the struggle against the grey enemies. In winter when the cattle are safe in their pens, the peasants put spokes in the hunters' wheel, but in summer when the wolves make daily raids on the herds and no hunter can do anything about it, they all yell for help. We are used to this, and so just offer the man a few extra rubles. When the wolf had been killed, Fedya would pay the peasant—with so many blows of his ski on his behind, while the others would laugh, urging him on, "Give him more, Fedya! Give him more!"

We settled the matter of the sledge and drove on our way. Where the road forked a man stood waving to us. We got out of the sledge and went up to him.

"Hurry up, they're waiting," he whispered.

From this moment, no smoking. To preclude a fit of smoker's coughing, each of us put a lump of sugar in his mouth. In other and more prosperous teams they collect fines for coughing. We weren't rich enough for this and then no one would dare cough anyway for

Fedya would chastise the culprit with his own hand: a fine in kind, as it were.

In our hurry we had left our skis behind and, wading through the deep snow, were soon out of breath; our heartbeats were so loud they echoed through the woods and bells rang in our ears.

My young companion started at a run as soon as he saw the flags. One could not help getting excited at these furtive preparations in the depths of the woods. Fedya's flags were quite unusual and well cut—like so many bright paper lanterns.

We went along the string of flags for about a verst, crossed the wolves' incoming tracks and finally saw "the silent man." His business was to keep silent and listen to the "criers." If the wolves rushed this way, he was to drive them towards the shooters because sometimes in their fright they were liable to jump right over the flags. The silent man got just as much fun out of it as any of the shooters: the final shot might depend on his alertness.

We reached the end of the flags and faced the fatal exit through which the wolves must pass. Dmitry Nikolayevich dug himself a hole in the snow opposite and stuck a few firs around him so that only his cap covered with a white handkerchief could be seen over the barricade. Fedya had a similar ambush about a hundred paces on. He removed a few flags to make a gap for us as well, drew a hack-saw from his leather case and built an ambush for each of us out of fir saplings. I believe he had made this saw himself, so it should work noiselessly, and his skis, too, were the only ones of their kind, made by himself as well. He had soaked them in something to prevent the snow from sticking in a thaw. He knew dozens of trades and was said to have built a shop with his own hands in the old days and gone bankrupt for selling goods to hunters on credit.

The wolves were splendidly *done*, but the criers had no proper leader. It was usually Fedya who led them but this time he had feared we would not be there on time and had taken up a position as one of the shooters. He soon realized that they were bungling it. Weren't his hands itching to get at them! I was not sure of my young companion on the left. A hunter can make a splendid show in snipe shooting when alone, and easily miss a wolf in company. A wolf will sometimes come within sixty paces. It is ten to one then that you can get him, but the way he is going he may come within ten paces of your neighbour if you hold your fire, and so you've got to control yourself and hold it. Sometimes another wolf will come out right behind the first, and you must let the first one go and shoot the second because it will confuse the first one and then you'll get him as well. But an inexperienced hunter may fire at the first and lose all chances with the second. This happens very often.

There was a haystack pole in front of me, and a fir on my left. My young companion stood at one side of the tree when the wolf came loping on the other, pausing as if dazzled by the white clearing, his hind legs sinking deep in the snow. His colour was queer against the white. I would not call it grey, no. . . . Suddenly he sank deeper, legs and all, he tried to struggle free, another shot rang out and he vanished in the snow, while I still stood wondering what colour he had been.

It was a large she-wolf, killed so neatly that the snow around was unruffled. She lay there as if alive, her muzzle on her forepaws, her ears cocked.

"A neat job," said Fedya, pleased. "But why did you fire a second time?"

The young man said nothing, though the reason was clear enough. A miss also called for a fine in kind, so it was always best to make doubly sure and take a second shot.

She was of a nondescript colour, grey with a yellowish tinge, but it was not at all the colour I had imagined as she stood proudly alive in the snow. I asked the young man what colour he had thought her to be.

"Green," he said.

Two of our men pulled out the pole, thrust it between the wolf's tied legs and carried it off the way they carry dead lions in the pictures of big game shooting in Central Africa. Fedya placed the wolf in the sledge in such a way that our gruesome load should frighten any horse in the road into the snow-drifts, thus clearing the way for the wolf-fighters.

My house stood perched on a hill above the lake, over that very road along which the endless timber carts were coming. That night, after the Feast of the Sun's Turn, an empty sledge train was returning from the station. The peasants had learned that the timber office would issue no more timber for three days because of the holiday, but since the railway went on working, they had decided to lay up a supply before-hand and then sledge it to the station throughout the new style Christmas.

The empty train of sledges was going back for more timber. The moon was new—a mere sliver—and it was very dark. I had managed to get a sturdy horse right after the hunt and rode home well ahead of the others to get a snack ready for them when they arrived. Listening to the shouting and cursing outside, I was thinking I had neglected to measure the depth of the snow that day, and made a rough estimate of it based on the growing fervour of the swearing. What matter really, so long as I could mark the daily movement of the planet by one sign or another and so complete the magic circle of its route that year. It is even better to record the movement not in figures but in images, for the figures remain in the observatories, while the people, ignorant of them, live in the immobile flatness. My images should penetrate the mind of the layman, who would sooner gauge the depth of the snow by an increase in the cursing on the road than by graduated figures.

"To think that we live in the age of aero-sleighs," I thought.

No sooner had this occurred to me, than there came such a tornado of curses from outside that I realized at once this could not be a mere gauge of snow-depth. Perhaps the wolves had sprung from a ditch along the road and dragged a dog from one of the sledges. I snatched up my gun and rushed down the hill. When my eyes got used to the dusk I saw a giant fighting the peasants, sending them sprawling into the snow. But the peasants were soon reinforced by a group from the next train, and things looked bad for the giant. He disappeared for a moment, but then re-emerged swinging a ski about until there was a magic circle around him. Everybody then saw that he was none other than the chief of our wolf-hunt, Fedya, and calmed down at once. The cause of the trouble had been the wolf's head sticking out of the sledge at the sight of which the first horse of the train had shied, the owner jumping off and starting a brawl. When Fedya went for him, the others came to his aid until it was a general free-for-all.

And so on that day of the Sun's Turn I made a record of the fact that many noses, too, were turned askew.

Father Wolves

The state wood stood guard at the edge of the field, its ears pricked. The field was watching and the forest listening. At the other edge of the field huddled the village of Ponikovka, like an old woman sitting and collecting into her bag everything that was to be seen in the fields, everything that was to be heard from the woods, and everything else she fancied she had seen or heard.

Many a bagful of forest odds and field ends had been collected by the old crone. Many a time we thrilled to old Spiridonovna's story of the terrible night she had spent in the woods, and marvelled at the wolves' strange custom of leaving tokens. Looking back at it now, the greatest wonder of the forest and field was Spiridonovna herself.

She was living with us in Ponikovka then. She was a sick-nanny, that is, she went from house to house, wherever a child happened to be ill, and stayed until it recovered.

Whenever one of the poor people's children fell ill, the gaunt old woman would appear in the doorway, and ask:

"Is the little soul still with us?"

The mother then could go back to her work with an easy mind, knowing that the child was in safe hands. No mother could be better and fonder than our nanny Spiridonovna. One day our Petya fell ill and we were altogether distraught. My wife sat at the bedside and I had to manage everything before work: fetch wood and water, do the shopping and everything else that needed doing. I had been neglecting my work lately and they were looking askance at me at the office.

But one morning I got out of bed to answer a knock at the door and there stood Spiridonovna asking:

"Is the little soul still with us?"

She relieved us of all our worries at once. When Petya had recovered a month later and word came that a child had fallen ill in Ponikovka, Spiridonovna said good-bye to our boy, parting with him like a mother seeing off her only son to war: she sobbed as if her heart would break. And soon she would be parting with another child with as much sorrow. That was why she was such a good nurse. Her mother's love was inexhaustible; as some women can grant love to many, Spiridonovna lavished hers on one child after another, and just when the little one got well and became her very own she had to part with it and go on to the next one. She was a wonderful woman, this nanny of ours, and I learned much from her during the month she was with us: she was always telling us one story or another.

It was New Year's Eve and an old man lay dying on the other side of the forest. There was no one with him in the hut but his orphaned grandchild. Left without the old man's care the baby had wailed itself into a fever. After late mass Spiridonovna was told that an old man and a baby were dying on the other side of the forest. It was customary to go to the graveyard after mass with offerings in memory of the deceased. Spiridonovna, too, baked some pies and took them along. The graveyard was very cramped—mound upon mound and stone upon stone. The graves could only be distinguished by the notches on the pines and sometimes there would be several notches on one tree. The graveyard ought to have been moved to another place long ago but everyone was used to this one; it was high ground and dry sand and the dear ones lay comfortably and the living could also comfortably come and have a memorial repast. The women set down their pies, the priest blessed them, the sacristan came and collected the offerings in his bag, and the sacristan's young pig came too to see what it could find, and this young pig had long been watched by a narrow jawed wolf-cub.

Spiridonovna was not a local woman and none of her relations were buried here, but she had a good cry just the same over the graves where the grief was freshest, and when the others had gone she crumbled her pies over these graves—she always saw to it that her offerings did not get into the sacristan's bag—and soon the birds came fluttering down to the crumbs. It was a joy to see them bathing in the sunbeams between the snow-laden pines. And Spiridonovna's heart knew blessed peace—and if her heart was filled with blessed peace, life was good enough for our nanny.

Meanwhile the young wolf kept crawling after the sacristan's pig along the ditch, until he nearly ran into the old nanny and, frightened out of his wits, dashed off across the fields and into the state woods. The fresh tracks across the snow were caught up at once by a party of hunters on skis who followed in hot pursuit. But suddenly the sky darkened and the snow fell thick and fast and the wind wiped away the footprints. It was only in the depths of the woods, where no wind could penetrate, that the tokens left by the wolves on the tree-stumps and bushes were not snowed under. And the wolves read these tokens in their wolfish way, left their own, and more wolves came, read and left their own in turn. And so the wolves read the news about their wolfish life and the life of man as it concerned their own. And the wolf-cub who had been chasing the sacristan's pig now wrote his tale over all the tree stumps.

As the sky darkened Spiridonovna's heart darkened too. She would not be able to get to the baby and it would surely die. She kept looking through her window anxiously to see if the blizzard had abated. There was a lull towards evening, but that helped little now, for she had to go right through the forest and the wolves were prowling in packs at night. Spiridonovna thought and thought what she ought to do when her neighbour came in with a child in her arms.

"Little darling," she said to the child. "Look through the window and tell me: should I go or not?"

As in olden times she believed that an innocent child could never tell a lie.

"Shall I lose my way or freeze or will the wolves harm me?"

"The wolves won't harm you, granny," the child said.

And so Spiridonovna knew she had go to. Her neighbour went to harness the bay horse, while the wolf-cub, who was watching the horse, scampered into the forest, leaving signs on the bushes saying that Spiridonovna was going to drive the bay through the woods that night.

The snow-storm blinded the eyes of the watchful field and stopped the ears of the alert forest, but the wolves knew after their own manner that the wind was sure to fall soon and even the moon to come out. The matron of the pack decided again to test the prowess of her big-headed mate and left her tokens in the forest calling everybody for a grand rally. Sniffing these signs thoughtfully, the wolves crept silently through the flaccid snow, gathering at the edge of the forest around their old ringleader.

They had chosen a good night for their gathering, the moon was soon out and the black mill in the field stood out clearly. The bushes of wormwood were so black against the white that the wolves at first mistook them for peasants coming out in the field.

The forest listened and heard a puppy yapping at the moon in distant Ponikovka. And the fiery wolfish eyes saw a low peasant sleigh skimming over the silvery white waves like a small boat, now riding high now sinking low, hurrying towards the black island of the mill. It passed the mill and ascended higher and higher. The old big-headed wolf, who brought up the rear of the pack, asked the she-wolf permission to go forward and stood ready for action.

Spiridonovna had dozed off, dreaming blissfully that she was already sitting on the stove rocking the child in her arms.

Spiridonovna took no notice of the wolves' tokens. She had tokens of her own and believed in them firmly, while her bay ran on and on. If you cannot see the road yourself, it is always best to trust your horse, who knows where the ground is firmest. If you tug at the reins you will be off the road at once, with never a chance of getting back.

And so the old nanny dozed on, dreaming that she had already arrived and was sitting on the stove-bed rocking the child in her arms, while the wolves were prowling the floor, and there were so many of them that they were climbing one over the other—higher and higher, almost reaching to the stove-bed.

But the child could not see the wolves and was getting better and better, and its cheeks turned apple red and it held out its tiny hands to her and called the old nanny Mother.

And the wolves were climbing higher and higher.

Spiridonovna flew into a rage; she was just about to hurl anything that came her way at them, but all at once thought better of it and holding the child tight threw herself right into the midst of the pack, sank to her knees, and bowed low to the wolves.

"Dear father wolves, I beg you not for my sake, but for the sake of my little angel, to go away and not frighten it any more. You are fathers yourselves, aren't you?"

What the wolves answered Spiridonovna did not hear for she woke up in a snow-drift and saw nothing but the bay's ears sticking out of the snow like a pair of horns.

The old wolf was nonplussed: the sleigh had appeared at the top of the hill and should have come straight down towards them. Instead it was gone! The Big Head wavered for a while and then, mighty though he was, surrendered his leadership to his wiser mate.

The she-wolf remembered a spot that was higher than theirs and emerging from the deeper gloom, she led the pack through the snows. They looked down and saw that fortunately the bay had missed the bridge and fallen into a drift. Their coats gleaming silver in the moonlight, they stole to the very edge and all glared down with their fiery eyes.

Spiridonovna was fussing about the sleigh, but the more she urged the bay on, the deeper he sank into the drift. She was about to get out on the road and try pulling the horse by the rein, when she saw the ring of burning eyes above her, and froze with horror.

The old wolf again resumed leadership. He planted his hind legs in the snow ready for a spring, but he, too, suddenly stood stock-still like Spiridonovna.

Wolves have a peculiar fear of the motionless which yet may be secreting life. They are even afraid of a newly-uprooted tree, and do not come close at once, but first try to propitiate the immobile unknown, and timidly approach it leaving their signs of esteem and awe.

Had a frozen and fragile twig snapped under her foot or had she stirred, they would have leapt at her and torn both her and the bay to shreds, but instead of running away she stepped forward, went down on her knees, and bowed low:

"Dear father wolves, I beg you not for my sake but for the sake of my little angel. Have pity, you are fathers too."

And so she remained bowed in the snow, and her stillness seemed even more puzzling and terrible to them.

The pack wavered, about to flee into the moon-lit space away from the dark unknown so motionless and yet so obviously alive. But the wise she-wolf came from behind her big-headed mate, sniffed carefully at the motionless body, left her token of respect and awe, and moved away keeping to the edge of the clearing. The others followed, each of them sniffing the immobile and leaving his mark of respect. And so, filing in the tracks of their leader, they left the fearsome spot.

Spiridonovna herself told us about her night with the wolves many a time, and we thrilled and marvelled at the custom of the wolves' tokens.

And the old nanny always ended her story with a good-humoured smile:

"And when I got up, my dears, I was drenched through."

The Mauve Sky

In December, if the sky is clouded, the twilight in the pine woods is weird and almost frightening. The sky turns mauve, hanging lower, slumping, and warning one to flee, for another, nonhuman life is about to begin in the forest.

As we hurried home retracing our path of the morning, we saw a hare's trail fresh in the snow. We walked a little farther and saw more tracks. So the hares, to whom our day was night and our night day, had left their homes to walk about.

And the awesome mauve sky of falling twilight was a radiant sunrise to them.

It was only four o'clock in the afternoon.

"It will be a long night," I said.

"The longest of all," said Yegor. "The hare will walk and walk and the peasants sleep and sleep."

Scent of Violets

Every time I go fox-hunting with a hound I say to myself that if I kill one I shall make sure to check on what Zvorikin, the famous naturalist and hunter, said in his remarkable book *Fox-Hunting*. I'm talking about that tiny gland at the root of a fox's tail which, according to Zvorikin, gives off a subtle scent of violets on a frosty day. As Zvorikin puts it, "for him the aroma of violets always consummates the graceful sport of fox-hunting." But it is a rare huntsman who has ever caught that smell: most of us are sure that the fox's tail smells simply of dog while some agree with Zvorikin out of sheer politeness. If I had not known Zvorikin to be an author who never said anything lightly, I would have compared his story with the tale of the naked king. But since Zvorikin had said it, it was as good as if I had said it myself. I am sure that Zvorikin really smelt the violets, and that is in itself an interesting biological fact. I wondered whether I should catch the scent myself.

The trouble is that a fox-hunt with a hound is not always successful: either the fox goes down a hole or it may lead the dogs so far away that one cannot catch up before dark. Personally, I considered myself lucky if I made my kill on the third day of hunting, usually it was the fourth, or even the fifth. And whenever I was determined to smell the violets I failed to make a kill, and when I finally did succeed I got so elated I forgot all about the violets. At last came a frosty day when I killed a fox and remembered.

It was a cold morning. There was a sliver of moon and all the stars were out when the three of us went to the forest with two dogs. My companions were the district legal adviser Y. and the local cinema pianist T., both excellent hunters. The pianist had his Kostroma hound Zalivai, a recent prize-winner, and I my true and unexcelled old Solovei. One dog, of course, would have been better than two of them unused to teamwork, but neither of us would leave his own at home. I mention this for the benefit of the less experienced: it is better to have one dog and at most one companion. There were foxes enough near our little town, but we knew them all, and they had all been so scared by our Tartarins and so experienced that they were impossible to get. We went down the high road for ten versts to find some foxes that had not been hunted. There was a fair on in town, a horse fair, it seemed, and as we walked along we saw a never ending stream of peasants coming down the road. Fortunately, we were still hidden by the darkness or else the peasants would have poked fun at us: they always do at hunters. We caught them unawares as we came out of the dark. The gleam of the moonlight on our gun barrels made their horses shy, which brought the inevitable string of curses. Sometimes, very rarely though, a quiet horse would go calmly by and the driver, dozing on the sledge, would open his eyes, at first startled, taking us for bandits, but then, guessing who we were, saying with nasty sweetness:

"Oh, hunters!"

This went on for a long time, and when the light came everybody greeted us with the same jibe:

"Hard times for hares!"

I was especially favoured:

"Don't waste your time, daddy."

It got on my nerves, and I asked the pianist:

"How many peasants are there?"

He answered, correctly enough:

"A million."

We reached our goal when it was just light enough to make out the tracks of a fox on the fresh snow, and unleashed the dogs right away. While Solovei followed the first trail, Zalivai found another and led the pianist away from us for the rest of the day. The lawyer and I went after Solovei, climbing to a considerable height. We came upon small heaps of sand, covered with snow, tossed up by the foxes digging their holes between the tree-stumps, and, sure enough, we soon discovered them. There was a perfect maze of tracks, and while Solovei was puzzling over them, we tried to review all the possible ways of escape and the best post to intercept the animal.

A rather broad stream all but encircled this hill of fox-holes. It was not yet frozen—a jet-black ribbon between the dazzling whiteness of the banks. On its other side stretched endless woods fading into the frozen mist. Across the stream lay a huge tree felled to make a bridge, cushioned with snow which was marked with a single track of fox's footprints running on into the woods. The tree lay embedded in some thick bushes on the other side, and a pair of bullfinches were pecking the burdock there. As soon as they had threshed enough seeds, the pretty birds came down and settled on the fresh snow, contrasting so sharply with everything else that wherever one looked, one's eye was bound to return to them with great pleasure. There must have been another crossing nearby, for we heard Solovei on the other side. As soon as he came to the single trail he gave voice and dashed on in full cry: the tracks must have been very fresh. The lawyer went down and took up a good post opposite the fallen tree and the two bullfinches. I hurried in another direction to look for the second crossing. Soon the barking was out of earshot but, while I was searching about, the chase looped back to the lawyer. I rushed to the top of the hill to get at least a bird's-eye view of the chase, and see where the fox could go if the lawyer failed to get it. The fox leapt into a large clearing, halted for an instant, looked round and went on in its easy graceful stride towards the fallen tree where the bull- finches were still busily threshing the burdock seeds. The bushes blocked the lawyer's view of the fox, but his position was very good and he was put on the alert by the baying of the hound. I watched, wondering which would happen first—the sudden flight of the bull- finches scared by the fox or the shot of my waiting comrade. But when the moment came I forgot all about the birds. The gun spoke just as the fox showed its muzzle through the bushes, and the bullet got it in the head. Mortally wounded, the animal kept leaping into the air and falling at almost the same spot.

We never knew how we flew across the foxes' bridge.

The fox's leaps were weaker and weaker and when the end came we went up to see how big it was.

There is no need to pity the animal, my kind-hearted readers, we're all due for it sooner or later, I for one am almost ready, and the only thing that worries me is that people might look at me and say in disappointment, "How small he was."

Indeed I have never seen a fox like this before—a huge ginger male, very old and with bad teeth.

We had no luck with the hares that day. Snow had been falling until just before morning, the trails must have been short, we did not pick up a single one. The brief wintry day flashed by unnoticed, and, before we knew it, it was dusk and we heard the pianist's horn, returned our own call and met again. He had got neither fox nor hare, but was glad of our success—he was a true hunter.

We went home cheerfully along the same highway. As ill luck would have it, the peasants were returning from the fair fortified with a drink or two, and as they saw the three of us with only one fox their greeting was invariably the same:

"Just one?"

We made no answer, but there was no end of them and it wore our patience thin.

"How many of them are there?" I asked.

"A million," the pianist said again.

We were fed up, and so we turned off the high road and found a track running parallel to it through the woods. We were so relieved we sat down on a fallen tree for a rest. The lawyer slipped the heavy fox from his shoulders and I suddenly remembered that I had always wanted to crown the graceful sport of fox-hunting with a sniff of violet scent. When I told my companions about it they all laughed. I then cited Zvorikin, an authority for every hunter, told them about the aromatic gland and even quoted the passage by heart. The pianist was convinced and as interested as I. The lawyer peered at me with professional scrutiny, trying to guess whether I was in earnest or just pulling his leg.

"Let me do it," the pianist volunteered.

He lifted up the fox's tail and sniffed in disgust.

"It smells just as you would expect an animal to smell there," he said.

A sceptical smile hovered on the lawyer's lips. I wanted to punish this doubting lawyer and, besides, let all of us get it equally from Zvorikin. I lifted the tail and took a purposely long time over my sniffing.

"You are mistaken, my dear fellow," I said very gravely. "You must have spoiled your sense of smell by smoking that awful tobacco of yours. I wouldn't say it actually smells of violets, but at any rate it's a very subtle aroma."

The ruse worked, and the lawyer, too, had a sniff.

"No," he said with a laugh. "You won't convince me; it smells foul—the king is naked."

A thin wall of trees separated our path from the high road with its endless stream of sledges. Wouldn't it be nice, we laughed, if all those peasants had seen us sniffing under the fox's tail. What would their drunken humour have prompted them to say then?

As the three of us sat drinking tea at my place that evening, I remembered Zvorikin resentfully and got his book out to show my friends that it was a recorded scientific fact. I read on, but when I came to the account of the aromatic gland, it appeared that it was not under, but above the root of the tail. That cushion which gave off the smell of violets on a frosty day was to be found above the tail just where the fox rests its nose when it curls up to sleep.

As we were pondering over this, the fox we had brought into the warm room began to smell so overpoweringly of dog that even our

three cigarettes were no match for it, let alone violets. We thought
of a million peasants meeting us along the highway, each shouting
the same:

"Hey, you hunters! You've sniffed the wrong spot!"

The Bears

1

Tigrik gave voice by a lair in one of the wildest corners of the
Olonets Province, Kargopolsky District, block 13 of Niemen Estate,
near the village of Zavondoshye. Pavel Vasilyevich Grigoryev, a peasant and part-time hunter, called Tigrik back with a soft whistle, cautiously skied a few paces and with a trained eye discerned the brow
of a rather large lair under the lee of an uprooted tree protecting it
from the north wind, with a clearing in front of it scantily overgrown
with slender fir-trees. Familiar with the habits of bears, and level-
minded as northerners generally are, Pavel passed by the lair to make
quite sure: the beast would not rise if he did not stop there. He had
not been mistaken: the spot was a breathing hole and the animal was
at home. He skied in a circle around the lair and criss-crossed his
tracks with his finger. By this he would know whether anyone had
come near and whether the bear was still at home. To throw poachers
of other people's lairs and any mischief-makers off the scent, he made
several sham circles nearby.

A few days later Tigrik again gave voice at a second lair in block
17 of the same estate. This time, the clearing was behind the upturned
tree sheltering the hole from the north wind. The animal, it appeared,
lay with his head eastward facing the dense coppice of firs. Skiing
around the lair Grigoryev nearly stumbled over the bear. At the last
moment he swerved some three paces off without rousing the animal.
As he checked his circles on one of the following days, he found
another abandoned lair of the same bear, obviously a huge beast. It
was this guess that made both lairs fall to us Moscow hunters and not
to the Vologda or the Arkhangelsk ones. The people from Vologda
offered fifty rubles apiece, but Pavel demanded nine rubles a pood
of the bear's weight, banking on its large size. Alternatively, he demanded sixty for a lair. Fortunately, while negotiations were on, it
occurred to Pavel to write to our Moscow branch.

That wave of bear scent that first struck the nostrils of Tigrik, then

the consciousness of Pavel Grigoryev of Zavondoshye, then of the
hunters of Vologda and then of Moscow would never have reached
me had I stayed in Zagorsk on that particular day. Luckily, I was in
Moscow settling various affairs, and more luckily still I was too tired
to run about any more. I still had to call on the editors of the *Ogonyok,*
but since their office was located on Strastnoi Boulevard and I was
then in Nikolskaya Street near the Hunter's Tea-House I thought I'd
drop in there for a minute. This tea-house where hunters sit talking
for hours has a wonderfully restful atmosphere. The old talk about
old times and the young about the future. Here, as nowhere else in
the world, they appreciate a writer who is genuinely keen on hunting
and nature. Although, who knows, these people might have made
the most enthusiastic readers of literature in general if their hunters'
hearts were not in the grip of nature's changing moods. I told an old
man about Gogol one day and presented him with some of his books.
They opened up a new world to him. How happy he was, this man
who had never heard of Gogol before, and how I envied him. But
there was another occasion on which he envied me.

I who had been a hunter all my life had never taken part in a bear-
hunt.

"How can that be?" The old man was amazed.

And then I was told about Pavel's first letter and promised to join
the party if agreement was reached. Thus, the bear's scent first caught
by Tigrik reached me at last.

From the tea-house I went to the *Ogonyok* and, talking to the editor,
let slip about the coming bear-hunt. The exaggerated importance
attributed to photography by the illustrated magazines is common
knowledge. Finally, affected by the chief editor's eagerness, I promised to take a photographer along with me.

"If you get a bear," he said, "I'll give you the cover page and a
splash!"

I did not understand and he had to explain that I would be put
on the front cover with the bear and that two full pages would be
given to snapshots of the hunt.

"You may bank on it!" he assured me as we parted. "I'll give you
the cover page and a splash!"

It is futile for an author to swear to the truth of his writings: such
oaths are always taken as part of a descriptive method. But I swear
by the oaths of beasts and not men that it was not myself I had in
mind when, in reply to a wire about the successful transactions with
Pavel, I telephoned the *Ogonyok* and told them to send a photogra-

pher. I was simply doing it for the hunters, knowing how they loved to be photographed with their guns and their catch. Everyone has seen such pictures! It turned out, however, that bear-hunters were men of a different cast. They were after bears and not images of them. To them an outsider and a photographer at that was a damnable nuisance. They were crushed when they heard about it, and only let him come out of respect for me. It was only towards the end of the hunt that we came to appreciate the photographer and saw he was no coward. But how could we see it earlier when the first thing he asked was whether he'd be able to use a ladder during the hunt and where he could get an outfit easy to run in? This kept the tea-house habitués rocking with laughter all day. The bear-hunters were reassured: the photographer, they thought, would take to his heels at the critical moment and they would be rid of him.

Soon afterwards, another letter arrived from Grigoryev in which he vaguely asked for sixty rubles for one lair and intimated that he would accept a weight rate on the other. A vague wire was sent in reply to his vague letter, but it did specifically state the day of our arrival. The business part was over, and the bears had been auctioned to the Moscow hunters, while our bear finder went on checking his circles, adding fresh tracks criss-crossed by his finger.

2

Some say that first impressions are always deceptive and check them again and again until they obliterate all the colours. Others, on the contrary, let themselves be carried away by their first impressions certain that the fresh colours are by no means less significant than the hard facts. As for myself, I can only speak of what made me marvel when I saw it for the first time. Why don't the animals in the zoo impress me enough to want to share my feelings with others? No matter how ingenuously realistic their background might be at the zoo, I am sure to catch some trifle to break the spell: the animal is not in its own element. If I had no more than a glimpse of a free bear crossing a real clearing in a real wood, I would certainly learn more than if I saw him pacing his cage at the zoo for days on end or led through the streets on a chain. It even seems to me that killing a bear in the Moscow Province would leave next to no impression: bears sometimes stray into our parts and make their lairs there, but such a thing is only a relic of the past—the bear has come there by mistake, he's out of his element.

But now I dropped everything in my eagerness to share with everyone my delight over this bright spring of light in the primeval northern forests where she-bears were delivering their young at this time, and the old and young bears lay half-dozing in anticipation of the coming warmth. I can see the gaunt but solid firs, the thick pillows of snow clinging to the rugged boughs, and the juniper bushes turned into fantastic white statues. I painted a whole collection of mental pictures of them. There was a queer faun-like old man, a sad-faced woman, sweet and graceful but carrying a heavy bag on her back, Maxim Gorky and Apollo, Sylvia and Olivia—they were all there in the wild woods buried in snow. I recognized them all and would not have tired of deciphering this wintry woodland story even for a hundred versts. What surprised me most was that on my return journey I recognized many of them anew and could tell by this how much longer we had to go. But the most fantastic image and yet the most realistic which stirred my blood, heart and mind was a dark brown head behind an uprooted snowbound tree. It was rising like the moon or the sun, as slowly, steadily and inevitably, while I stood a few steps away taking aim.

A full moon, a Venus as large as my fist, the Great Bear and the entire vaultful of stars made the snow so bright that we could distinguish the tracks not only of foxes, hares and squirrels, but even the delicate lacy prints left by white partridges and black grouse. This made our seven-verst trip from the station to the village of Zavondoshye a sheer pleasure. Pavel's numerous family slept on the floor in the two rooms, with Tigrik stepping nonchalantly over young and old alike. The air was stifling. Our knock was followed by some brisk action. The sleeping children were moved to the other room, the table was cleared and a samovar brought in. In an undertone the photographer asked the host, "Pavel Vasilyevich, where is the toilet please?"

This was the first chasm that yawned between us—men rashly, senselessly committed to danger, and the man who had come to photograph and later display it. Our conversation was dull shop talk to him, though our lives depended on it as he was later to see. I had no carbine and carried my twenty-calibre smoothbore instead. From the books I knew that it was not safe to face a bear with such a weapon, but I had somehow felt sure that I was not to be the leading character and would have to fire only in case of emergency. Everything turned out differently though. I was made the master of one lair, while the master of the other was the shooting gallery marksman who was also the treasurer of our society, a Czech by birth. I had happened to take him for a Greek at first—may he forgive me—and I shall call him "Greek" in this story. He too was a novice in bear-hunting, but was armed with a carbine of the most formidable type. The third man was an old bear-hunter, but acted only as manager, protector and instructor. We called him "Godfather."

"I would not face the lair with calibre twenty," he said, "but never mind! We'll cover you."

It was awkward to back out now. One could make a kill with a small bullet too, of course, but every age has its own technique and its own skilled performer. If the prevailing weapon for hunting bears had been a bow-spear and I was skilled in the art of handling it, I would not have thought it strange at all: the bunglers perish and the skilful fall only by accident. But this was the age of carbines and express bullets and only the amateurs came out with shotguns.

I was behind the times. Most aggravating was the thought that I was to be neither the first to use the carbine nor the last to kill a bear with a bow-spear. Neither fish nor fowl nor good red herring, so to say.

"Perhaps I could just look on when you take the first lair?" I suggested. "I could then help with the second."

"Of course," said the Godfather, "but there may be no second. We may just scare him away, and who is going to write about the hunt then? And what will you say if you're only a witness? You'll be sorry afterwards."

I agreed. Godfather suggested that Greek should allow me the first shot without casting lots, and excellent friend that he was, he agreed without demur.

We slept for only two or three hours. A shrewd diplomat in ursine affairs, Godfather waited till the very last moment when everything was ready and the horses harnessed before he tackled Pavel about the vague terms of his letter. We were to pay 60 rubles for each lair or 9 rubles for every pood of bear meat. In case we let the bear get away, we should have to pay sixty. We refused this cash basis for one lair and weight basis for the other.

Pavel pondered deeply and then pronounced:

"Both lairs on the weight rate."

Godfather was overjoyed because that meant that the bears were really big.

Just before we set off Pavel reminded us to provide a fourth cart. "Who for?"

Pavel looked at Godfather significantly, the old man understood and ordered the cart to be brought around at once. To say what it was for out loud was an unlucky omen: the fourth cart was for the bear which I was to kill.

The photographer then demanded a ladder and he was so insistent that we were convinced he really needed one. The ladder was brought with the fourth cart. The photographer was a lucky fellow.

Rarely had I seen such a glowing spring day before. The taiga was shot through with golden rays and there were tracks of lynxes, foxes, hares, squirrels, partridges, and blackcock everywhere. I did not know which way to look. The snow was so fragrant in the sun!

It was not a road but the tracks of someone else's sledge we were following. Every now and then we got jammed amid the trees. Avalanches touched off by the sweep of the bow harnesses fell on our heads. The photographer begged that we should stop before every snowy arch. Whenever we did, Godfather would grumble:

"Another show!"

There was something grave about the forest. There was not a single track or path. Wherever there was a ski trail our driver could tell exactly whose it was and why. We came to a stop when we found our own ski trail left by the bear finder to mark the first lair. We got out, shed our sheepskins and got on our skis. Godfather and Greek made their carbines ready and my heart missed a beat as I took out my own dapper weapon. Trying to kill a bear with that, and the first shot was mine!

Our maestro was irrepressible.

"Turn your face to the sun! I can't see it. Push your hat up!"

"Don't pay any attention to him!" Godfather whispered to me. "Let's keep after Pavel. I'll tell him talking is forbidden."

I no longer saw the beauty of the northern forest shining in azure and gold. The only thing that worried me now was not to snap a twig. This one verst seemed like ten. At last we crossed the magic circle. Without pausing Pavel pointed to the north with hand and beard towards the thicket where the bear slept. We may have been very near, but it was our purpose to skirt the thicket and find ourselves facing the lair in a clearing. How desperately I wished just then that something would happen at the last moment and I should not have to fire that day but just look on. Tomorrow I'd do it gladly. . . . It was like being back at school and drawing an examination card, feeling that everything had gone clean out of my head and praying in all earnest: "Deliver me, oh Lord. . . ." Besides, I felt that all my hunting stories were being put to the test. What if it turned out that I was just a fraud—a hunter on paper! What was more, if I was a fraud of a hunter I was sure to be a fraud of a writer as well.

At last, the clearing with the sparse firs came into view. The bear finder halted and *pointed*.

His job was done. I would have to pay for the lair now if the bear got away. As I advanced he stepped back. I moved forward with Godfather on my left and Greek on my right. There were a few firs ahead and an uprooted tree with a dark hole, about the size of a hat, beneath it.

What a nuisance were fingers freezing from contact with the steel. I couldn't warm them either, because the bear might appear at any moment now. Twenty paces from the hole, we paused for a short whispered council. Greek circled the lair from the right in case the bear had another exit. Godfather took up a position on my left to shoot if I missed or merely wounded the bear and he rushed on me.

Now I stood facing the bear. I had to get off my skis and trample the snow under me. As soon as I tried it, I sank into the snow to my waist. I could not even see the hole now. What was I to do? I had never read about such a contingency and no one had ever told me either. I was trapped. The bear would get away and I would not even see him. Godfather whispered from above, urging me to get to the fir-trees. What next! Those trees were only 7 or 8 paces from the hole. Still, I obeyed and struggled on. When the trees were behind me, I looked up at my instructor, who nodded approvingly. My feet then began to trample the snow of their own accord, making stoops which I climbed until I could see the hole again. I saw now that the dark ginger spot which had looked like a bear from afar was nothing more than an upturned root of the fallen tree. I was in position now—and free to act. Now who had taught me all that? What was happening behind me I did not know. I had even forgotten about the photographer and his ladder. We were heading for a climax, tension grew. Greek lost his head and did not seem to know that it was his job to guard the rear of the lair. Godfather was furiously waving his hands and whispering frantically, his face splotched with white and red. Greek at last got the idea and moved backwards.

How clearly I understood then that the inner struggle between the proud free man and the coward was inevitable and needful for it's the coward in us that puts us to the test. One could not talk oneself into bravery as one could not stop the heart from thumping more and more violently. I thought it would burst in a moment, but then came the line beyond which there is no struggle, the coward was vanquished and I turned into a mechanism with the precision of a steel spring in a clock.

The line was drawn when I heard Godfather's loud clear words: "There he is!"

Something stirred near the roots. I waited, my gun steady. The ears appeared, as I'd seen them in the zoo, they were rising slowly, steadily and inevitably. Then came the curly line between the ears. I needed the line between the eyes and felt that at this rate I would have a long wait. It was like aiming at the rising moon.

Could all this great stillness have occupied a mere earthly second? When I heard a voice behind me in this great interval of silence, it seemed to be coming from a long-forgotten world where people were swarming about as in an ant-hill. It was the voice of our photographer from his perch on the ladder:

"Could you stand a little to the left!" he admonished Godfather.

"Go to hell!" said the well-bred and even refined old man.

It was just then that the long-awaited line between the eyes appeared—I'd seen it in the zoo too. My heart stopped. My mind and will and all my senses, my very soul, were concentrated in my index finger on the trigger, and it acted of its own accord.

It must have happened when the bear was slowly stretching himself after his winter crouch, preparing for a leap. My shot brought his forepaws and belly into view. Then, he fell over backwards and slid back into the lair.

It was all over and the winter was fine and lovely again. It was so warm and beautiful! Could summer ever be as wonderful?

The bear was dragged out. He was not very big. But what did it matter after all? Godfather embraced me and congratulated me on my first lair. Greek came up beaming. Godfather turned and begged the photographer to forgive him. He was a brave fellow, for he had stood on his ladder just behind me with no weapon at all. Somehow we felt that we owed him an apology, and he, taking full advantage of our contrition, made us turn to the right, to the left, bend down or take aim to his heart's content. We were like wax in his hands for a while. All he wanted to do now was photograph the lair, something which could not be done unless we chopped down a fir-tree, the same tree that had probably made the bear choose this spot for his lair, the same tree that had served me as a beacon when I had sunk into the deep snow and felt that my sportsmanship was on trial.

"No, we can't do that," we said and did not let him cut down the tree.

3

We discussed our battle with the bear until late at night, though the whole thing had taken only a few seconds. Nor did we care for the drink usual after a winter day's hunting. This abstinence, I think, explained the origin of the desire for drink, arising as it did out of the necessity to create illusion when one was not really satisfied. It was pleasant to get up early next morning, to wake my comrades and listen to the bear finder's story about the second bear, a huge one in his opinion. He should have known, since he had passed some three steps from the lair and saw the animal lying unconcealed between two fir-trees, protected by an uprooted tree alone. But what pleased me most of all just now was not that this bear was so huge and lying openly, but that I had done my bit and could thereafter take up the role of witness and observer.

"Let's see how you make out, young man!" I taunted Greek.

Godfather smiled in his beard. He had been to scores of bear-hunts, and never had two cases been alike: it was different each time and very often it was the man cast for the least role who had to play the leading one. His words remained with me until after we arrived on the spot and began loading our guns. A perfectly puerile day-dream got hold of my imagination. I saw Greek, as inexperienced as I, failing to inflict a mortal wound. The huge animal would be about to trample him down, but I would come up and make the kill with two shots between his eyes. I even resolved to save my shots for this horrible emergency.

We were skiing in a new formation now. The bear finder in the lead of course, next came Greek, the master of the lair, then God-father, then I, followed by two of Pavel's boys, one carrying the ladder and the other the rope for our prospective kill. Today, relieved of my heavy responsibility, I was able to notice that the cones on one of the firs were ablaze in the sun and looked like golden balls. On the very top a small bird perched against the azure splendour of the spring of light. The tracks here were mostly those of the lynx. The bear and the lynx often appear in the same spots. Perhaps they seek each other on purpose.

Suddenly the bear finder signalled us to halt. He looked worried. Perhaps the bear had got away?

Pavel vanished in the thicket and then appeared again. We moved on hesitatingly. It was whispered that he had lost his circle. The driving snow had probably swept his finger marks, and now he could not distinguish the true circle from the false ones. We thought that the lair was still quite far away, and so our weapons were kept on the safety-catches. It turned out that we were mistaken, for Pavel had lost not the circle but the lair. We were already well within the circle.

We passed through the dense coppice and found ourselves in a clearing. Pavel, Greek and Godfather were already crossing it in single file. I only had two more fir-trees to go past. I even noticed the uprooted tree and had I looked a little lower I would surely have seen. . . . As it was, all three of us passed the spot unsuspecting.

A dead yellow crownless tree rose in the clearing. My last ordinary thought was: It's strange that Pavel can't find his circle by this conspicuous tree. Just at that moment Pavel halted and gestured us to do the same. We thought that he had found his circle at last, while actually he had been looking for the lair itself. He must have thought that we were all ready, for when he suddenly recognized the spot, he pointed to me. We were so unimpressed with his finding the circle that Godfather did not even turn his head. I did stop though, and the lad with the ladder behind me stopped as well.

"Look, look!" I heard his alarmed whisper.

Later we measured the distance. The uprooted tree was exactly three paces from the spot where I stood. The roar came from somewhere under me—in two bursts. Put into sound it was the thing I had seen yesterday when something stirred in the dark hole under the roots of the tree, and slowly began to assume the shape of a wild beast's head. I got off my skis and sank in the snow. My gun seemed to leap to my shoulder of its own accord, and what I saw over the sights was quite different from what could be seen with the ordinary eye. My head was clear. This was just like yesterday and I must do the same. The same long stillness swelling in intensity. The familiar hairy line between the ears was becoming wider and wider, now the bead-like eyes would appear. Everything would work out beautifully, as yesterday, because my arm was firmer than any steel. But, suddenly, instead of widening, the line of the forehead receded, the nose appeared and a very thick throat. What was I to do? Nobody had told me where I was to aim, and the throat was so thick! Most probably I ought mentally to divide it in two and aim at the middle. It often happens that the hunter has no time to think and presses the trigger with the absurd last hope: "Come what may!" My index finger did not have the whole of me concentrated on it this time, it did not press the trigger of its own accord but followed my vague order: "Come what may!"

4

It seemed to me that it was all happening on a great expanse and that my friends were far away. Later we checked on one another and established that Godfather had stood four paces from me and Greek six or seven from him. Why had not Godfather, since he was so near, fired at the temple of the bear when he was rising? He knew better than anyone else that firing at the neck I could hit the backbone only by sheer accident. And besides, my bullet might fail to break the main ridge. One convulsive movement of the dying animal's paw would have been enough to knock off my head. My fate had been sealed. And yet he had not fired. I was puzzled.

That is the most surprising thing about hunting wild beasts. As the boy with the ladder told us, he had noticed the bear by the movement of its paw: one of the paws covering the bear's eyes in sleep began to slip aside and that was when he whispered, "Look, look!" And all that followed: the bear climbing out of its lair and towering over me, buried in the snow, and sinking back baring his throat, and all my thoughts and actions up to pressing the trigger did not give Godfather enough time to turn in his tracks and take aim. Greek had seen everything, but the cart drivers who had been following us out of curiosity had stood right opposite him, behind the bear. He had seen the men over his sights and hesitated.

It's only a split second a man needs to remove his safety-catch. Yet when I pressed the trigger and no shot followed, and I glanced at the safety-catch and removed it, it was too late: the broad hind of the animal was wobbling swiftly away through the dense trees. I discharged both barrels at random, with no mind to the trees. There must have been a gap in the trees somewhere in front of Greek, because he—an excellent shot—took his chance and fired twice. I saw the animal, a huge wound in its left side, swerve abruptly and start across the clearing towards Greek. Godfather could not see this and I shouted to him, "Shoot, he's turned!" Godfather stepped forward, saw the whole thing and fired. The animal now turned on him. In that split second its head was clearly visible to Greek, who fired, and the bear dropped in its tracks, an immobile dark brown splash.

And all of it, from beginning to end, did not take more than a few seconds, incredible as it may sound. White as a sheet, Godfather came up to me and said, "Why, you're quite white!" Greek said the same to Godfather, though he was just as white as we were. None of us had felt a speck of fear, for the cowards in us must have been still trudging behind us when we were facing the suddenly aroused beast, and had only just arrived when it was all over. Why else should we have turned pale now? This cold bravery of ours reminded me of a moment of mortal danger during the Civil War. Then too I had felt the same cold tranquillity as if I had taken a double aspirin to relieve a headache.

What surprised me most of all was that Pavel had turned pale too. He did not know the difference between ordinary and express bullets. Nor could he have seen the cart drivers behind the bear. He had implicitly believed in our experience and never doubted that we would not let the bear escape once he had led us to the lair. Here was the thing as I saw it: he was to have shown us the lair and cared for nothing else after that. But what did happen was that he lost the lair, the animal rose, and was going off! Had the bear escaped twelve poods and a half at nine rubles a pood would have gone off with him: a hundred and twelve rubles and fifty kopeks. Look at it in terms of stone-hard corn bread, a house full of kids, twenty versts on skis to check the lair, and the ever present, joyous thought that it was a big and costly beast that was lying there. Well, my brave Moscow friends, you would turn pale too if such a thing happened to you.

5

Our habit of clinging to past experience and the desire to talk about it without end stems, of course, from the general tendency of human nature to hold the moment and glory in it all life long. Besides, we were all interested in the problem from a personal point of view. True, the last bullet had belonged to Greek, but it was clear that the beast was in a daze and would have collapsed soon anyway. The question, therefore, was which one of us had dealt the mortal wound.

Each reconstructed the scene according to his secret wish, trying to conceal it from his neighbour and make concessions to him. We learned something by comparing notes, but only a post-mortem would establish what part each one of us had actually played.

With great difficulty we dragged the bear out of the forest and carted him to the village. In the morning we brought him into the house and began on the post-mortem when he had thawed. I am sorry I have no photos of this. The bear lay sprawled with his hind paws reaching to the icon corner and his forepaws stretched back over his head like gigantic hairy arms about to seize the big Russian stove and hurl it at me. It was humiliating to feel one's frailty before that powerful body. My imagination carried me back to those infinitely distant ages when man was as monstrously strong and fought the bear as an equal. In the Stone Age our hairy forebears hunted the mammoth, and now the last woodland giant was being hunted by a bookkeeper, a dog fancier, a writer and a photographer.

The knife began its task of parting the dark coat.

"This would make a good photo," I said to the photographer.

"It's an unpleasant sight," he said and went away.

The first look at his wound in the left side, the injury which had made him swerve into the clearing where I saw him with a huge red splotch in his side, made it obvious that my bullets had had nothing to do with it. They must have lodged in some of the trees. The wound was caused by an express bullet. The burst had broken three ribs, and a splinter of the bone was found in the heart. Several fragments of the bullet were found in the heart too, and the lungs were perforated. To think that the animal could have run for forty paces with such injuries! What if he had turned on the cart drivers instead of on us? Greek had inflicted this injury with one of his first shots. Godfather's bullet had penetrated under the left shoulder-blade, had burst after contact with the ribs in the right side and completely destroyed the right lung. Even then, the bear had run on for several paces. It was Greek's last bullet—after he had reloaded his carbine —that had hit the head and felled the bear. The physiologists may not believe me, but that was how it was. The vitality of the bear was astonishing. Yet Pavel assured me that a bear like this with short fat claws never attacked cattle. I had never attached much importance to this current belief that only the bears with long claws fell upon cattle. But one thing was clear: not all bears attacked herds. Most of them dug up ant-hills, licked wild strawberries and other berries, gathered honey and unearthed various roots. What knowledge of the

woods and what effort a bear must expend to build such mighty
muscles out of such poor material, while Greek, who had no mind
for anything but his bookkeeping, had borrowed a handful of express
bullets from a friend and let them fly, with no idea, possibly, of how
they were made. And the man who had designed them probably
never even learned to let them fly and never cared. All he was concerned with was to design them, and the bookkeeper—to let them
fly. The bear, on the other hand, had gathered unto himself all the
vital forces of the forest and this probably explained his vitality.

We were a little sorry for the bear of course, but then he had made
us famous, really famous.

Our fame began back in the woods where the bears live and fre-
quently blunder upon people in the raspberry bushes. Young and
old poured out to see the bear; they looked at it, talked about it and
touched it in a way that made it difficult to dismiss the thought that
this passionate interest was a remnant of the ancient bear cult. It was
only a few days before that I had read the latest articles by learned
hunters asserting that it was impossible to kill a bear with a bow-spear,
that it had never happened and that such stories were mere legends.
I, too, was beginning to believe it and the origin of this legend fascinated me. But now the old people brought out a rusty bow-spear
and showed how it was handled in the old days. When a bear rose,
they threw a fur cap into his mouth to slow his attack, one of them
then plunged a spear into him and another struck at his nape with
an axe. One Yermosha knew more than the others about spear hunting, but he happened to be away in a lumber camp: this Yermosha
not only knew how to hunt with a spear, he had once actually whipped
a bear to death with his belt. Quite a big bear too.

The hubbub in the village did not cease until we left for the station.
The station-master turned out to be a new man on the job and was
flabbergasted when I suggested shipping the bear unpacked. He fum-
bled through his books for reference and, deciding that a slaughtered
bear belonged to the category of slaughtered cattle, demanded that
the carcass be submitted for vet inspection. But then Godfather stepped
in and told the man how things were done in the old days: the hunter
carried the bear to Moscow unpacked and his fame grew from station
to station. In Moscow the bear was taken on an open sledge to Lawrence, the famous furrier and taxidermist, where the hunter had the
bear either stuffed or made a rug of. Lawrence then invited the
hunter to witness the skinning to see where the bullet hit.

"The hunting cost a lot of money in those days," said Godfather, "and there was nothing but fame in it. What good would it have done to ship the bear all trussed up?"

Upon this, the young official relented and dictated a statement to me:

"I hereby send this bear in an unpacked state and assume responsibility for all the consequences thereof."

The bear did not come to life on the way and there were no consequences except that in Vologda they stole my wallet with the luggage check, and I was afraid that the resulting formalities would take so long that the bear would be eaten up by the warehouse rats. I copied the number on the check for the second bear, took my friends with me as witnesses and went to the local militia station. There was nobody there. There was no station-master either, or anyone on duty or even a weight checker. They had all joined the crowd gathered around the bear. A cartman came and we carried the bear to the sledge. Scores of youngsters had followed the sledge to the station, some acquaintances had seen us through their windows, while others had met us on the street. By three o'clock the whole town was talking of nothing but bear. Friends and strangers telephoned me, asking all sorts of questions and heaping congratulations upon me.

I have been living on my street for three years and everybody knows me, yet when I'm giving my address I always say, "Next door to Melkov." Now Melkov is a horse-flayer. When I hire a cab in the district, I always say, "Drive to Melkov's."

But now that I have killed a bear, the youngsters all make way for me wherever I go. One day I overheard some people chatting as they sat on a bench before their house.

"Even a hen would fly at you when it's angry, but just think what a bear must be like!"

Then I overheard another snatch of talk:

"Where does the horse-flayer live?"

"Next door to the hunter."

"You mean the one who killed the bear?"

"Yes, that's the man. He's a writer, known all over the Moscow Province."

And they were right as I see it now. How infinitely small is the span of the written word as compared with the thousands of years in which man fought the bear.